HUMAN LIFE

HUMAN LIFE

A Biblical Perspective
for Bioethics

J. ROBERT NELSON

Fortress Press   Philadelphia

Library of Congress Cataloging in Publication Data

Nelson, J. Robert (John Robert), 1920–
   Human life.

   Includes bibliographical references and index.
   1. Life—Biblical teaching—Addresses, essays, lectures.   2. Bioethics—Addresses, essays, lectures. I. Title.
BS680.L5N44   1984   233   83–48140
ISBN 0–8006–1754–1 (pbk.)

K367E83   Printed in the United States of America   1–1754

To my writer son
William John (B. J.) Nelson

CONTENTS

PREFACE

To the ultimate questions we finite humans can give only proximate answers. The simple question, What is life? is an ultimate one. There are three main avenues of approximation to its elusive solution. One is the road of biological investigation, including within it the accruing findings of biochemistry and biophysics. The second is the path of philosophy—critical reflection and imaginative speculation on the observed phenomena of all living organisms. The third is the way of theology—reasoned interpretation of the wisdom of faith, which lays a certain claim to a source in divine revelation.

In past centuries and millennia, men and women have leisurely pondered the question of life's nature and meaning for a variety of reasons; among them were scientific curiosity, awe before unknown forces and destiny, and yearning for meaning to existence. In the latter half of the present century, however, the need has become increasingly urgent for intelligent and responsible persons to possess a conception of life. If that conception cannot ultimately be true, it needs at least to be of practical use in thinking through the life-and-death problems that science, technology, and social change are rapidly creating for us.

The new field of bioethics, closely related to medical ethics, is one in which the most pressing need is felt for a workable conception of life. Which of the three avenues of knowledge is most appropriate? For an atheist, only two; for a believer in the God who creates and reveals, all three. The failure, or perhaps even the inability, of thinkers of the three ways to communicate with one another is notorious. Nor can there be realistic expectation that such communication will soon become possible—much less that wide agreement will be reached. We who choose to walk the way of theology know what barriers separate our minds from others.

In 1981 I had the honor of talking with a prominent micro-
biologist, the mention of whose name here would arouse the read-
er's suspicion of my ostentation. His research is directed toward
what the popular idiom calls "creating life" from elementary
chemicals. After an hour's serious conversation, it became evident that our respective thoughts on "life" ran on parallel tracks,
never to meet. In such experiences it is tempting to feel despair
over ever seeing the intersection of the science, philosophy, and
theology of life. But some intuitive force enables us to resist that
despair. We keep seeking, if not a synthesis, at least an intelligible
and interacting discussion of this most essential but fugitive issue.

My first real awareness of that intuition was felt in 1968 while
taking part in an international consultation on human experimentation. It was convened by Hans-Ruedi Weber at the Ecumenical
Institute, Château de Bossey, Celigny, Switzerland. That event
allowed me to meet persons already involved in this quest, notably Edmund D. Pellegrino, M.D. The "theses" set forth here
in chapter 5 were first sketched at that consultation and published
in *Experiments with Man* (1969). Thereafter I began teaching a
seminar called "The Meaning of 'Life' in Bioethics," and I now
feel obliged to thank those students at Boston University and the
Vancouver School of Theology who contributed more than they
knew to my own thinking. An invitation by Professor Howard E.
Hunter to deliver the Russell Lecture at Tufts University occasioned the earliest draft of chapter 1. Of much value in this process
were the personal associations and research opportunities I experienced at the Kennedy Institute of Ethics, Georgetown University, and those I enjoyed as a consultant to the President's
Commission for the Study of Ethical Problems in Medicine and
Biomedical and Behavioral Research in the area of genetic engineering.

Later drafts of chapter 1 were published by the Christian Medical Commission of the World Council of Churches in Geneva
(1982). Portions of chapters 3 and 4 appeared in *The Journal of
Medicine and Philosophy* (vol. 3, no. 2, 1978) and the book *Orthodox Theology and Diakonia,* edited by Demetrios Constantelos
(1981). A short form of chapter 6 was published in *Hospital Progress* (vol. 63, no. 12, 1982). For helpful criticism of chapter 2 I

am especially indebted to Professor Diana Hall, historian of biology of Boston University. Chapter 3 was read (and approved!) by Professor Isaac Franck of the Kennedy Institute of Ethics; chapter 4 by Professor Krister Stendahl of Harvard Divinity School; chapter 5 by many students of my seminar; and chapter 6 by fellow members of the Panel on Bioethics of the National Council of Churches and by a number of recognized religious ethicists whose comments were solicited by Executive Director Alexander M. Capron of the President's Commission in Washington, D.C. To all these constructive critics and teachers I am genuinely grateful.

Gratitude is here expressed to the Reverend Wesley E. Amundson for carefully compiling the indexes of this book.

1

WHERE THERE'S HOPE
THERE'S LIFE

APPRAISING THE HUMAN CONDITION

In a perfect society of human beings there would be unambiguous consistency in the rule of rationality and morality. To speculate on such perfection is the occupation of utopian thinkers and dreamers. They justify their efforts to describe the sociology of utopia by saying that we will never attain a good life for all if we do not keep striving for the best.

If we were now living in a consistently rational society, we would know how to avoid everything that corrupts our health and deprives each person of a satisfying livelihood. We would eat and drink what is known to be good for our bodies while avoiding whatever tends to outrage our metabolic systems. All the machines and devices of our exploding technology would be designed and used to provide satisfactions with maximum safety, both to human beings and the whole impersonal environment. By good sense and reasonable agreement, groups, classes, and races of each nation would maintain a stable and equitable economic order within a just political system; and the nations of the world, concurring on the restraints of reason, would cooperate without armaments or hostility. Human society in all dimensions would thus be governed by rationality.

In a consistently moral society, moreover, we would know how to control suspicions, animosities, and passions which cause people to cheat, injure, and destroy one another. Summoned to act beyond the bounds of a calmly reasoned morality of justice and mutual respect, we would willingly incur, as occasion required, inconvenience and discomfort, and even danger and deprivation to ourselves in order to defend, preserve, and enhance the lives

1

of others. In all respects we would be charitable and generous toward everyone, and especially toward the weak and defenseless members of this most agreeable society.

Until that best of all rational and moral social systems is achieved, however, we must continue to live within structures and situations that barely deserve the adjective "good." Being consistent in neither morality nor rationality, these structures are characterized mainly by ignorance, avarice, duplicity, prejudice, and self-interest. Widespread injuries to both physical and spiritual health, as well as the premature destruction of lives, are tolerated with equanimity by the majority who luckily manage to escape them. The need and pain, the exploitation and death of those who are weak fail to arouse ample remedies and continue to be ignored.

So gloomy an appraisal of the human condition is not shared by all, to be sure. Many millions of people are generally satisfied with their experiences of living and with the social situations in which they live. They are decent, friendly, nice persons. Somehow the furies of distress and tragedy pass them by. Congratulate them! They are the fortunate few in the midst of the maledicted many. Statistics comparing people by the hundreds of millions are not needed to demonstrate the imbalance between the blessed and the wretched of the earth. If we are not numbered among the battered, however, we have daily reminders of their plagued existence. Before our eyes, thanks to instant communications, passes the melancholy parade of newsworthy events of evil consequence. And the journalistic descriptions of abject conditions of humanity acquaint readers (those who take time) with the tyranny, terrorism, and torture that are the political counterparts of disease, destitution, and death.

"These things just ought not to be," says the educated, liberal, humanitarian optimist. Look at the human achievements of the past two centuries—the literacy, democracy, science, industrial technology, medicine, and the United Nations with its complex of international organizations. These should surely have reduced to tolerable levels by now the quantity of human suffering and despair. Every indicator shows that the human race has entered a new era in history.

With all the technological marvels increasingly made available
to the world's rich minority, the most appropriate designation of
the era has been said to be "the century of the common man."
Whether common or uncommon, each woman and man and child
of this minority has a better chance today, on average, of realizing
an extended and satisfying life than did his or her ancestors. But
are the odds favorable enough to bring genuine hope to the poor
majority? It does not seem so. And are the benefits of civilization
sufficiently abundant and available to mitigate the sense of pathos
and alarm? Not yet.

ENHANCING LIFE AND DEBASING LIFE

Having entered this new era of human evolution and history,
in which scientists and technicians can compete with nature in
shaping the species Homo sapiens, we members of the race are
now confronted by a demanding question. Will we use all our
resources, energy, and newly acquired skills to enhance the life
of all people? Or will we by malice, carelessness, or default allow
or cause life to be debased?

Survival and Hope

Often in these days it is said that the primary question is just
that of human survival. The threats to the whole, or most, of the
human race are neither fictional nor hypothetical. More than three
decades after the invention and military use of the deadly atomic
bomb—decades of wild proliferation rather than firm control—
many scientists and political savants are convinced that we live
on borrowed, and possibly brief, time. The apocalyptic vision of
a barren, radioactive, peopleless planet haunts the minds of young
people especially. It is they, or their children, they fear, who may
be the victims of instant cremation or inexorable, agonized death.
Albert Einstein's life and achievement have been feted enthusi-
astically and universally; but the sober warning he gave to the
nations in 1945 has gone unheeded. The international balance of
terror may not be sustained indefinitely. It is foolish complacently
to think that not only the human race but the planet Earth is
beyond jeopardy. Yet it is also a mark of craven hopelessness to

3

be resigned to the inevitable cataclysm. What we hope for as human beings, despite all obvious danger, is more than mere survival. Animals may be content to survive; humans cannot be. That is the essential distinction between thinking human beings and unreflective animals: animals survive whereas human beings hope.

If the object of hope is not just survival, then what is it? The object has always been the same, whether in primal or highly sophisticated culture, namely a good life, better than is generally known now, a life enhanced, a life of quality. Yet this answer begs the question, What kinds of life and living are good?

There is an irony of history here. Just when it seems for the first time conceivable that most persons on earth might have a chance for that enhanced life which deserves to be called "good," there has come a tidal wave of debasement and destructiveness. There have always been two kinds of destroyers of human life: first, natural calamities and disease; second, other human beings. To reduce the deadly effects of drought, tornado, earthquake, and epidemic disease is a matter of ingenuity and good sense, aided suddenly and marvelously in this century by scientific and medical technology. To restrain men and women from harming themselves and hurting one another is an essentially moral problem, perennial and universal. It is *the* moral problem with respect to which, we know from reliable sources, insufficient progress is being achieved.

Wasting Life

One thing boggles the mind when we ponder the intrinsic value of a single human life in relation to the total of humanity. That is the sheer quantity of individual lives that we can only judge to have been wasted. To be wasted means to fail to fulfill one's purpose, to perish before one's potentiality has become actuality. This thought begs another question, Is there purpose in living? This is the most profoundly perplexing philosophical and religious question. For human beings it cannot be adequately answered in terms of biological continuity, species survival, and evolution.

So far as we can judge, the purpose of their existence is being achieved when dragonflies, swordfish, and caribou manage to eat enough to strengthen them to reproduce their kind. In fulfilling this purpose, individual specimens of many species may experience pleasure as they forage, ingest, digest, and do what comes naturally with their sexual organs to bring a new generation into being. In numerous ways, moreover, animals of all kinds—amoeba, snails, fish, insects, birds, mammals—play their specialized roles in ecological systems, thus contributing to the continuity of the processes of nature. They perform acts of such prodigious exertion of strength and accuracy of movement, often involving huge expanses of earth, that we can scarcely believe some accounts told by observing zoologists and naturalists. These animals also show remarkable ability to organize their habitats, build nests, and lay away supplies of food for themselves and their offspring.

Animals that have been domesticated by humans obviously have acquired and developed some modes of behavior that their masters and trainers consider good. Related to this behavior is their manifestation of a sense of expectancy at the master's coming, at feeding time, or at the opening of the door that allows them freedom to run. Horses, dogs, and trained dolphins and whales demonstrate a sensitivity that approximates and resembles human hope.

Hypersensitivity to a smell, a temperature, or a chemical in their natural state and even responsiveness to magnetic fields about them are now supposed, or shown, to be the causes of the wonders of animal behavior. The older theories of instinct have lost some of their credibility. Nevertheless, it remains apparently true that the basic purpose of each animal's existence is to preserve its species. Failure means eventual extinction of its kind. We human beings deplore the threat of extinction of the animals we most admire—the tigers, condors, whales. But we may reasonably ask whether it is conceivable that individual members of these species can reflect on what the planet would be like without them, and whether they have hope for themselves or their species for a better future.

For a man or woman to brood on the prospect of a peopleless earth is neither unlikely nor uncommon. Though we may believe that our living selves transcend the confines of time and space, we know ("something tells us") that human survival is intrinsic to the existence of the earth, and that our hopes for a good fulfillment of our longings are not fatuous. In the last analysis, of course, this belief or intuition depends upon acceptance of a metaphysical, or divine, reality from which self-consciousness derives, and to which such values as what we call "meaning and purpose" are ascribed. Sigmund Freud admitted this elusive mystery in his *Civilization and Its Discontents*: "Nobody talks about the purpose of the life of animals, unless perhaps it may be supposed to lie in being of service to man . . . only religion can answer the questions of the purpose of life . . . the idea of life having a purpose stands and falls with the religious system."[1] The corollary of Freud's assertion is that the burden of proof rests upon the materialists and philosophical naturalists to show the basis for the phenomenon of hope.

Thoughts on human wastage are accentuated by comparison to the easily observable aspect of all biological reproduction, namely the prodigality of germ plasm. Considering all forms of animal life, including the human, the fact of this spendthrift habit of nature is both amazing and appalling. If all their progeny survived, a pair of sparrows would within ten years produce twenty-four million. How many sperm cells are generated to fertilize how many eggs? How many eggs in certain species are needed to produce one specimen that can survive into maturity? Not the sands of the desert but the atoms of the earth are suitable comparisons to the numbers involved.

If our thinking moves beyond the molecular quality of germ plasm and living tissue to the realm of consciousness—feeling, mind, thought—the range of possible phenomena becomes virtually infinite. What are the boundless resources and potentialities of mental processes in the individual? Thoughts, affections, dreams, words spoken and heard, significant actions, memories, hopes—of these there is no end. So wastage means not only the inadvertent or premature cessation of bodily life, but the deprivation of these uncountable possibilities of human experience. And among these are the potential contributions that can help society, or collective humanity, realize those hopes for the "meaningful" and "purposeful" life of all. How many "village

Hampdens" and "mute, inglorious Miltons" lie in disintegration under the rude tombstones? asked the popular, brooding poet of the eighteenth century, Thomas Gray.[2] (He was himself the only one of a large family who survived infancy.) Or how many unrecognized Confuciuses, unknown Newtons, immature Mozarts, or unidentified Edisons are among those millions who might have been or who, for various nefarious reasons, suffered untimely termination? Of course, this glass of reflection can be reversed in respect to moral good by asking the same questions about potential mass murderers and destroyers of life. In either case, we are ruminating on the tantalizing thoughts of what might have been if human affairs were otherwise.

The analogy of wastefulness as drawn between humanity and the rest of the animal kingdom is neither forced nor far-fetched, even though the number of four billion living persons compared to many species is relatively small. If we could assume optimistically that each one who matures beyond infancy has hope of a long and happy life, how many are actually able to experience that satisfaction? Statistics and percentages need not be cited to demonstrate what we all know of the human population. In spite of the upward surge of life expectancy, especially in Europe and North America, vast numbers of lives come abruptly and prematurely to an end. Longevity itself is not necessarily equated with a good and happy life, but almost without exception the realization of one's potential for happiness and satisfaction requires adequate years. A death is called "untimely" because it ends one's life before the realization of what normally may be called fulfillment. This duration need not be "threescore years and ten," but certainly must exceed childhood and adolescence. A concert program included works of Henry Purcell, W. A. Mozart, and Franz Schubert. These three composers had each died by the age of thirty-five. Were their lives thus unfulfilled? Hardly! Nevertheless, these are the rare exceptions. It is with the masses of mortality that we are concerned; the unknown and unsung millions who can say "Our life is unwelcome, our death Unmentioned in 'The Times.' "[3]

The inadvertent deaths due to natural disasters are reported incessantly in the news media. We note the headlines and half-hear the broadcaster's laconic announcements of statistics. But we are hardly moved to genuine sympathy or sorrow or alarm. Since 1945 earthquakes have killed more than a million persons. They always seem to occur in remote places of the globe, however. Guatemalans, Turks, Romanians, Filipinos, Chinese, and Italians have been among the recent major victims. Americans, with the exception of some on the West Coast, feel neither empathy nor fear. Persons of a cynical mind dismiss the news with a shrug. "This is the way nature controls population," they say. "Suppose everyone lived to be seventy—what chaos!" To the contrary, however remote they may seem, these are sad and deplorable instances of human wastage.

Recklessness with health and safety is another, and greater, cause of throwing away the goodness of life and living. Our appetites outrage our digestive and cardiovascular systems. Uncontrolled thirst for alcohol destroys our livers. Despite the incontrovertible medical evidence of the lethal effects of tobacco and all the vigorous warnings by public health officials, cigarette sales keep mounting and lungs deteriorating. Automobile traffic safety rules seem only meant to be broken by tens of thousands of drivers, especially when they are daydreaming, delayed, or drunk. But there is nothing accidental about an "accident" due to driver stupidity or inebriation.

If disaster and recklessness account for many hapless deaths, the deliberate wastage of life by acts of killing is even more rampant. Just as we consciously produce masses of domestic waste, industrial waste, and now nuclear and bacterial waste—the sum of which we cannot dispose of with efficiency and safety—so the calculated actions with intent to kill cause human waste. To apply a new word, human life has become "biodegradable."

A hundred wars, great and small, have been fought *since* 1945, a date often referred to as "the end of the war." In these hundred or more armed conflicts at least ten million children and adults have been killed, often in the cruelest fashion. Some of these wars have been intended literally as genocide—an effort to annihilate a whole nation or people. In civil wars the killings are fratricide. And all the wars are collective forms of homicide.

Meanwhile the number of individual homicides keeps mounting

in most countries where crimes are reported, the United States being far in the lead. Murders within families or domestic households are astonishingly numerous, and their causes are often of a petty, trivial nature. Simple explanations of cause or motive are seldom valid, but evidence mounts to show that the nightly diet of the bloodiest violence on cinema and television screens lessens the inhibitions to kill. The lack of legal controls on guns, and the failure of society at large to change the economic and psychological conditions that contribute to such assaults are the negative contributions to homicide.

Even suicide is losing the aura of shame and scandal, especially among younger persons, and is looked upon as the easy escape from pain of body or torment of mind.

Genocide, fratricide, homicide, suicide—these are the overt and visible killings. Because they are witnessed, experienced, or at least seen on television or reported in news media, many people are sensitive to them. They arouse responses of anger, horror, fear, sympathy, and fleeting resolves to do something to curtail them. More widespread, however, is the disposition of people to become passively inured to such human wastage of life.

There is another "-cide" to this morbid picture. It is invisible to all but a few and therefore easy to disregard. Moreover, people are divided in their judgment and sensibility as to whether it is truly human death. This is feticide, the killing of the human fetus, or unborn child, of whatever stage of gestation. Conservative official estimates now set the figure at more than one million abortions annually in the United States. Due to inaccurate reporting, or concealment by furtive women and unscrupulous physicians, only conjecture suggests that the annual toll for the world may rise to forty or fifty million. Of course, it is said that "feticide" is a biased, emotionally charged word. If the impersonal phrase "terminating a pregnancy" or the clinical-legal phrase "exteriorate the product of conception" is used instead, this irritating and perplexing cause of death could be removed from the category of wastage of life. Many are content to put it in an entirely different category from human death. Thus, annual reports show that in every one hundred thousand abortions there are only four deaths. Only four? Or one hundred thousand and four?

Is not humanity caught in an imponderable and vicious circle? If a "timely" death may be determined at about seventy years on average, the devaluing of life can be affected equally by either too many or too few "untimely" deaths. The extreme instances of the rising and falling of national or global population seem to illustrate this strange dilemma. In times of catastrophic decline of population, the value of an individual life is debased. Just imagine the incomparable Black Death, or bubonic plague, of the fourteenth century, or the recurring famines following drought and the ravages of locusts, or the slaughter by enemy troops of inhabitants of cities under the invaders' swords, or obliteration bombing, and genocidal killings in death camps—these are the conditions in which the spectacle of dying persons and accumulating corpses numbs the senses to what is normally considered the precious miracle of an individual life. Then what is the worth of one human being when thousands are suffering extinction? As the numbers of survivors decrease during these boundary situations of existence, so does the concern for life.

Ironically a superpopulation has the same effect. China and India are the notable examples. Always more populous than any other country, they accept with resigned equanimity the apparent inevitability of high rates of infant mortality along with the recurring famines and epidemics of disease. The casual saying "life is cheap" was invented by Westerners to describe the Asian's acceptance of untimely and uncountable deaths. Now, within a generation's time, just a momentary period in their five-thousand-year histories, China and India have learned health care. Babies survive infancy, diseases are checked and cured, food distribution is regulated. So China passes the one billion mark and India exceeds six hundred million. Do better health and longevity enhance respect for life's value? Or do the inconceivable numbers of people not induce even more readily the general notion that many lives are expendable?

There is an extraordinary mystery here. It is like a double helix with two spirals of humanity. One twists downward in numbers as millions die too soon; the other twists upward as millions are conceived, born, and survive. Yet, through the strands of each spiral the sensitivity to life's worth flows only downward.

And this double helix leads at its base to the truly vicious circle, where indifferent attitudes affect the callous wastage of life, even as the waste intensifies the indifference. Can a thoughtful and sensitive person pondering this mystery avoid becoming pessimistic?

Pessimism about life's value is not a recent mood brought on by the heightened anxieties of this century. It is a perennial perspective, both ancient and contemporary. Much of the most durable and poignant literature in all languages, especially poetry and tragic drama, has been written by persons addicted to brooding over the frustrations and injustices, the brevity and vanity of existence. That such pessimism is not a novelty is attested by the one who remarked, over three thousand years ago, that "there is nothing new under the sun." Koheleth, the world-weary preacher, concluded that the day of death is better than the day of birth, and that all of life is mere "vanity and a striving after the wind" (Eccles. 4:16; 7:l). Poor old Job, too, sitting on the ashes of his contrition and burning with painful sores, was the paradigm of numerous men and women in all places and times who have cursed, as he did, the day of their birth (Job 10:18). Even Second Isaiah, the noble prophet of hope in a divine purpose, mused that "all flesh is grass," which fades and withers into nothingness (Isa. 40:6–8). This Hebraic patrimony of pessimism is also conveyed through some of the great psalms which tell of the transiency and pain of living. Through the ages, too, the seers and poets of Greece, India, and China have held up for our pensive reflection the dark and menacing side of life's mystery. In modern times, from the "walking shadow" of Shakespeare's *Macbeth* to Eliot's "hollow men with headpieces filled with straw," the sombre side of life and living has found abundant literary expression, matched as well by the visual arts.

Between the melancholy brooding of poets and the hard, cynical enmity toward life which is widespread today, however, there is a profound difference. Melancholia is a sensitive person's tormented struggle with the manifest imperfections of life as lived. Cynicism is the utter indifference to the wastage of human values and callous disregard for the preservation, protection, and enhancement of life.

Callousness Toward Life

A perplexing yet revealing question should be put to all of us who regard ourselves as the urbane, civilized, and reasonable men and women of this decade. Are we more callous toward human life than our predecessors in history were? *That* we are callous to a large degree is hard to dispute. That we have *become*, by and large, more insensitive to suffering and death can be argued in differing ways. In a retrospective scanning of textbook history we read about homicidal events which were utterly horrendous. We may wonder whether there were any compassionate advocates of the slave laborers who died of exhaustion and unattended disease while building the pyramids and colossal temples or while digging into deep rock to excavate the tombs of ancient Egypt. Who besides the victims themselves protested the sportive killing of innocents in the "superbowls," the amphitheaters of the Roman Empire? Was the rectitude or legitimacy of torture in ancient China ever challenged by the serene Confucian philosophers because of their sympathy for the wretches on whose bodies the famously ingenious, exquisite assaults were made? Timur-i-Leng, or Tamurlaine, led ravaging armies that freely slaughtered tens of thousands of citizens from the border of China to Russia, India, and Syria. He is remembered symbolically for his mountain of a million skulls, a number which is probably not an exaggeration. How "un-Christian" that was! And yet it was the Christian Pope Innocent III who turned the French crusaders upon their own neighbors, the heretical Cathari of Languedoc. Having been given the papal promise of perpetual indulgence of their sins if they served forty days in the war, during just one day in 1209 they butchered and burned twenty-five-thousand persons in the walled city of Béziers. Thus allegedly they earned their own salvation while destroying the victims for *theirs*.

The history of atrocity includes numberless examples of human depravity. Ivan called the Terrible earned his sobriquet in Russia by, among many memorable acts, driving men into the forest to be pursued and killed for sport, as though they were deer or boar. He caused his spitted enemies to be turned slowly over a low fire, apparently with as little reluctance or remorse as that shown by Vlad the Impaler ("Count Dracula") toward the twenty-thousand Turks wriggling and dying on sharpened stakes. In the city-states of Renaissance Italy, as courtliness and the visual arts were flourishing, it was commonplace to behold mayhem and carnage in public places or find, in the morning, bodies floating downstream. And still we wonder: Where were the defenders of human life? Who were *not* callous to the killings? Who were those sensitive persons who could not accept with equanimity the tolls of infant mortality and epidemic as well as exploitation of serfs and menial workers unto their early deaths?

Advancing into modern history, we shudder at written descriptions of the agony and death of millions of Africans, ripped from their roots, and perishing on slave ships bound for America. The idealistic French Revolution, proclaiming "the rights of man . . . liberty, equality, fraternity," culminated in a reign of such terror in Paris and Lyon that it was no mere figure of speech to say that blood filled the gutters. Since then, two hundred years of wars have brought untimely, terrible deaths to tens of millions of persons, civilian as well as military. And the crowning affronts to any idea of a humane respect for human life were the genocidal executions of Armenians by Turks in 1915, of Jews by Nazis a generation later, and of Cambodians by their own people.

Historians, especially popular ones, are obviously more disposed to record the atrocities and cite the savageries of tyrannical potentates and warring nations than to recollect the evidence of humane care and costly compassion. Such information as we possess is probably insufficient to permit a generalization about the extent and intensity of concerns for life's value in these eras of the past. Thus, an accurate comparison of the prevailing mood of today with the dominant attitudes of past history seems impossible.

If it cannot be demonstrated statistically that the present degree of humaneness is less than in other eras of history, we nevertheless know enough about the modern history of Europe, the United Kingdom, and North America to make some judgments. Consider only the past century and a half.

Humanitarian Countermovements

The last excesses of feudal cruelty merged into the new industrial exploitation, and crimes and wars continued with the use of more technically efficient killing devices. Nevertheless, during the nineteenth century there arose a strong countervailing movement of compassion for the weak and defenseless. Voluntary initiatives, often impelled by religious faith in life's dignity and worth, led to a heightened sensitivity to care for children. For orphans homes were established where the cruelties and horrors described by Charles Dickens were changed to humane care. Adoptive agencies and foster-parent programs replaced the atrocious foundling homes, where infanticide, both passive and active, had ended the lives of tens of thousands of unwanted babies. Child-labor laws removed ten-year-olds from factories and coal mines; universal compulsory education put them in schools; and public-health programs inoculated them against the familiar, lethal diseases of the passing era. This was likewise a century of building private hospitals and establishing social-service and welfare agencies, supported by free contributions of money and labor.

Movements also arose to secure the proper rights of women, of ethnic minorities, of prisoners, and the poverty-stricken, not because of some abstract ideal of democratic justice, but from a strong religious commitment to the essential goodness of human life and the need to protect it. With plenty of notable exceptions, then, there was an ascending mood of compassion on these continents. The voluntary programs were the vanguard of the legislation in state and national jurisdictions, tending inexorably toward the enhancement of life for all citizens.

This humanitarian crosscurrent in the river of history has been of benefit to millions who might otherwise have lived in degradation, disease, and with relatively few years. During the same period, however, despite legal prohibitions, there were great numbers of abortions. The crudity of methods frequently led to serious mutilation of women, and many died along with the child they had decided to avoid. The concerns that prompted anti-abortion laws included: the protection, reputation, and health of women,

14

the humanity of the fetus, and the public respect for the emerging medical profession.[4] Few physicians, legislators, moralists, or religious leaders of the nineteenth century held that abortions were morally unambiguous or that they were wholly within the discretionary judgment of a distressed woman.

If abortions were discussed in hushed tones, people were much more apprehensive about euthanasia. To kill means to kill; to kill intentionally means murder. Most people of reason failed to see any alternative to that formula. Physicians, nurses, and hospital personnel were aware of the fact that decisions were being made to withhold treatment from critically ill patients, especially the elderly; but this knowledge was seldom revealed to the public. Many a physician or nurse wrapped the facts in the soiled linen of a bad conscience, doctoring the death records to avoid exposure. The uninhibited advocates of euthanasia legislation became publicly vocal in the 1930s, evoking from the public a horrified response to what was euphemistically called mercy killing.

There prevailed, in summary, a wide consensus in feeling, theory, and law that human life was inviolable and protectable from its beginning to its natural ending and at all points in between. Any exceptions to this position in the medical and social sphere, or in legislative and judicial action, were thought to be due to wrong judgment, deplorable living conditions, or just original sin.

Life vs. Quality of Life

So it was thought until about 1965. No single happening of that year marked the sudden swerving of public opinion, although one can theorize about the precipitating or catalytic cause. That it *did* happen at about that time is now, in retrospect, obvious. The life-affirming conviction was being redirected in the minds of those who came to think that a certain political ideology arising from recognition of the population crunch, or that an undefined value called "quality of life," was more important than any human life itself.

Why did this happen? A number of factors may be noted as likely causes for the seismic shift in popular mentality.

1. The imprint of totalitarianism in Europe has been pressed on the minds of men and women in many lands. While some felt

only revulsion against the barbarous practices of the armies, secret police, torturers, and executioners of both Fascist and Communist states, others have accepted implicitly the notion of superior and inferior people and the total power of the state over all. It was Nazi doctrine that all people can be divided into two categories: Aryan and non-Aryan. Only the former deserved full human respect. Or the Nazis agreed with the Communists that people who were useless, inconvenient, or hostile to the state were *Lebensunwerten*, unworthy of life, and thus suitably doomed to *Vernichtung*, annihilation, by efficient systematic programs of murder.[5] It is now horrible not only to contemplate the numbers of Jews, Gypsies, genetically irregular, and mentally ill who were killed, but also to consider the brutality of the emotionless executioners and the indifference of many who knew of the murders. For it was the case with many ordinary citizens, the "good people," whether bourgeoisie or comrades, that they accepted without sympathy or outrage the rumors and news of these atrocities. The exposures since the end of the war in 1945 have not prevented neofascist movements from continuing in Europe and the United States, or in some South American countries, where repression, torture, and politically motivated murder continue. And regardless of political spectra from right to left, the gulags and labor camps of the Soviet Union have their counterparts, according to Amnesty International, in at least sixty countries today.

2. Disdain for the lives of "lesser breeds" was certainly spread by America's involvement in costly military campaigns on the Asian continent. It was fulsomely reported and illustrated how American fighting men lumped together and despised all Asian people, whether Koreans of north or south, Vietnamese of north or south, Chinese or Laotians. "I'm sorry about that!" was the expression muttered by the more notorious soldiers in Vietnam as they sprayed civilians with machine-gun bullets and napalm. But after all, these were only "gooks," not real human beings. Americans "out there" as well as those "back home," motivated by such a racist attitude, could speak blandly of the "daily body count" with scarcely a thought or urging of human sympathy.

3. The demographers' fears of population explosion began to be shared by the public at large during the sixties. This could be expressed in the formula: Fecundity + Longevity − Food Supply = Catastrophe. Some became zealous evangelists for zero population growth, arguing that the survival of the human race depends upon rigorous limiting of childbirth. The reasonable and practical way of control is family planning, a laudable concept that presupposes implicitly the integrity of two threatened institutions: marriage and family. Development and marketing of the contraceptive pill, along with other devices of varying effectiveness and safety, have greatly inhibited procreation both within marriages and by extramarital intercourse. However, advocates of zero population growth are justly concerned that not enough wives, husbands, and transient lovers of the world have the good sense and prudence, or even the knowledge and means, to practice contraception. Indeed, many others follow the official moral instruction of the Roman Catholic and Orthodox churches that forbids contraception by artificial means. And men and women of Africa, Asia, and the Third World diaspora in the West resolutely reject the propaganda of family planners, which they interpret to be a white population's genocidal threat against other races. As apprehension has developed over the slow and unsatisfying success of birth-control programs, the once unmentionable method is increasingly mentioned and practiced—abortion either as backup to contraception or as a chosen mode of preventing birth. The postwar legalization and advocacy of abortion in Japan was officially presented to the Japanese people as a national eugenics plan.[6] Many Japanese women and men found the euphemism devious and the program itself abhorrent; people in other countries were shocked by the news of hundreds of thousands of abortions even while recognizing the personal reasons other than population control that are used to justify them. Today, fewer are shocked as they have seen the United States and European nations follow the Japanese lead. In the People's Republic of China the need to control population growth has led, first, to economic inducements and, next, to mandatory requirements for women to have abortions. If a vestige of moral revulsion remains

over the annual megadeaths of fetuses, it is covered, in the minds of many, by the satisfaction of knowing that the "population apocalypse" has been to some extent postponed.

It is hardly to be wondered, then, that people's attention has moved from the unborn to newborn infants with genetic disorders, to the mentally and physically deformed or infirm; and respectable people now speak without hesitation or apology of the need for morally and legally justifiable infanticide.[7] The line next runs to the senile men and women, the hopelessly infirm in illness and old age, people who are incapable of having normal personal relations with others and who burden family and public financial resources as well as scarce medical resources. In the name of population control, economic scarcity, or the "quality of life," these can also be marked for painless elimination. From infanticide to senicide!

The extreme reaches of such thinking account for both fantasies and actual cases which are lurid and sensational. Extrapolating from the instances of individuals and small numbers, some persons who think most broadly about the Malthusian theory of a global debacle caused by the disproportion of people and food supply are able to argue for an international application of "triage"—writing off classes of people and whole countries that are apparently doomed to starvation, and limiting assistance only to those that can be made self-sustaining.[8]

Mass starvation, euthanasia, and abortion have one thing in common—the cessation of life. At whatever stage of development, with whatever quantum of "quality," with whatever personal involvement of affection and care in the lives of their families and friends, millions die annually of these preventable causes. How are people accepting this current and foretold situation? With strong words and angrily raised fists of protest? With tears? With a sad resignation to inevitability? With a sense of guilt? Or with disinterest, equanimity, and even approval? Callousness toward the waste and loss of human life is measured by the answers to such questions.

4. Some widely accepted judgments about the state of Western culture today can be added to the factors already described as evident causes of the chilling toward life's intrinsic value. We

know that to a large extent our society has become bereft of authentically human and personal qualities. What the North Carolina novelist Thomas Wolfe styled "the million-footed manswarm" appears as a mass society of think-alike, act-alike units. Among them are large numbers of persons whose philosophy is called by psychologists "the new narcissism" and by moralists "the new hedonism." This may mean for them a respect for life all right—but only for *my* life. There is a lowering of consciousness about all human well-being except that of the first person singular. Each ego has established its own cult of personality— itself. When the senses of persons committed to such solipsism are bombarded incessantly by particles of homicidal violence and other inhuman outrages, whether as daily news or as fiction, it is inevitable that their imagining and fantasy will seek an escape from any humane and costly concern for the welfare or very existence of others. In perfect congruence with this endemic egoism, television entertainment has turned Nazi S.S. troops into comic-strip clowns, and movies have made the Mafiosi appear to be adventurous heroes. The practitioners of the cruelest sadism run helter-skelter through the mass media to everyone's nervous amusement or disgust, making mockery of the stark reality that torturing of suspected detainees and political prisoners has become in our time an accepted practice to a degree exceeding that of the maligned Dark Ages and ancient paganism.

Mass media thus tell mass man of mass murders and massive assaults on human dignity and life. But the hedonistic devotees of the pleasure principle and the "autophilic" searchers for self-fulfillment are unmoved. If not moved to pity and appropriate action, however, they can be moved to irritation by people who are, by contrast, vocal and expressive about their sensitivity and anxiety. A name or an epithet suffices to put down and dismiss the advocates of oppressed and weak persons, the opponents of handguns, capital punishment, and war. To call them "bleeding hearts" and ridicule them as "do-gooders" convey the cynics' frigid conception of human life. Then compassion is called cowardice, and sensitivity senility. Outrage is out of place.

If it is true, after all, that the populated world is at best a domesticated human zoo and at worst a jungle of human predators,[9]

19

it pays to be indifferent to violations of human dignity and the imminent inevitability of death. The best counsel is to turn away one's face and avoid involvement. Thus, impassive or timid spectators do not interfere with robberies, assaults, and murders in daylight and in public places, or incur even the slight risks involved in helping victims of highway accidents or persons who are drowning. Such incidents are reported frequently, while many of the same order are probably never observed. So if the morning television news shows plastic bombs exploding in a public gathering, or a firing squad executing both their orders and their victims, or a shoot-out between police and a homicidal maniac, it is likely that the evening entertainment will be twice as gory as the real events.

How culpable are the people who assume an indifferent, insensitive, unsympathetic attitude toward widespread impairment and destruction of life? Are they personally responsible for their disaffection? Are they so bestial and depraved by nature that they are merely manifesting what is otherwise hidden under the thin veneer of a humanized culture? Are altruism and compassion really foreign to our primordial and essential nature? Here we stare again into the mysterious abyss of evil in human behavior, wondering without ever learning why it is found there.

One component of the elusive answer to such questions stands out in the foregoing discussion of reasons for callousness toward life. It is the susceptibility of persons to mental conditioning by influences working upon them externally. Few seem to have the capacity to resist and withstand the forces of vulgarized ideologies or popularized tastes and prejudices. Manipulation of minds is big business, whether it be for the purpose of advancing political beliefs, selling cigarettes and detergents, propagating religions, or debasing life's value for the sake of sensate entertainment, commercial profit, or military aggrandizement. To whatever degree any of us can swim against the stream of commercial advertising and political sloganeering, we still know that we *are* being manipulated and conditioned by what we cannot avoid hearing, seeing, or experiencing. It is frightening to discover how readily we capitulate, even against our better judgment and will.

A fair analogy to the way one becomes callous toward the life and death of other people is the experience of a middle-class person who is suddenly immersed in a situation of utter destitution. One goes to India, let us say, as a volunteer teacher. Despite the fascinating beauty and glories of that ancient land and people, the initial impact of the sights of human degradation is overwhelming, terrifying, and depressing. After a day of walking in the back streets of Bombay or Calcutta, or in some dusty villages, visitors from a privileged country feel a compulsion to escape. Being of good nature and inclined toward philanthropy and ameliorating actions, they become an easy mark for leprous beggars and pitiable though clever confidence men. They feel wretched in the bleak knowledge that the best of charitable offerings will not make the tiniest scratch in the surface of India's economic need. And though impressed and inspired by the example of Mother Teresa, the Nobel laureate of the Calcutta slums, the courage is probably lacking to follow her example. What shall such visitors do? For a while the sense of guilt, helplessness, and misery increases; but then something unexpected happens. After six weeks or so, they awaken to the realization that their sensitivity to abject poverty and diseased disfigurement has receded. Sights have become familiar and no longer wound their conscience. And the tender skin around their affections has turned to callous tissue.

One need not go to India, however, for this is a familiar experience for all who work and live in the constant presence of degradation, horror, and death. Not just the visiting bourgeoisie, but the poor themselves become inured to their condition. Many physicians and medical personnel learn that they must exclude undue sympathy for their suffering patients and also overcome revulsion at the sight of carnage. Yet, that necessary professional coolness can turn into a shoulder-shrugging coldness. This can happen to anyone, and often does.

Exalting Death over Life

When human life is debased and negated for the deliberate reason of self-centeredness, callousness, or nihilism, what is the corollary of such an attitude? It is the morbid disposition to exalt death over life. Some would insist that the current popular interest in death is not a sign of morbidity but of maturity. It represents, they claim, a widely held intention to abandon both undue anxiety and inordinate sentimentality about death in favor of a calm and reasonable realism. The claim is debatable, however. From a different perspective, the numerous books, articles, panel discussions, college seminars, and symposia on thanatology indicate a cavalier attitude toward life and a view of death that is both frivolous and morbid. Which is the true estimate of the phenomenon?

For a decade or more, death has had no holiday from constant scrutiny and analysis. The intense public interest in "death and dying" owes much to the pioneering researches and perceptive observations of Elisabeth Kübler-Ross, the title of whose famous book imprinted an indelible non sequitur upon our common speech: in human experience, of course, dying comes before death.[10] Her widely read books followed upon other persons' earlier studies and exposés of bizarre and costly funeral practices in America as well as the strangely pagan ideas about death which account for them. She went behind the problems posed by American ways of handling corpses to the intimate experience of persons in their final hours and moments. By listening to the whispered words of dying men and women and observing their facial and bodily responses to the dreadful power that was depriving them of life, she delineated the recurring patterns. The seriousness of such inquiry and the attendant desire to give beneficial assistance and consolation to the dying persons cannot be questioned.

Her good work has been continued by many others. However, it has been perverted in part by people who have lost personal concern for the dying and have become intensely fascinated by death itself. Perhaps this has been only a side effect of two kinds of serious inquiry: first, the responsible, scientific attempt to define death and its implications, which are biological, medical, and political matters; and second, the questioning of death's mystery, which at the last is a metaphysical and theological issue. It is this side effect that constitutes the faddish craze. It takes, in turn, two forms: one frivolous, the other morbid. Neither of them is healthy for the individual or society.

Frivolity acclaims death as a lovely event. It suggests a doctrine of *kalathanasia*—beautiful death. Death is the end of suffering and pain, which in the hedonistic mentality are the worst of evils. It may be the fortunate extinction of a troublesome life ("Out, out brief candle," cries Macbeth) or the tranquil one-way passing into a higher spiritual world. Just as the mortician's cosmetic art makes the corpse look nicer than in real life, so the verbal cosmetics of the enthusiasts would make death seem a pleasant prospect. Thus we can be urged, as it is said, "to die with style" whether gamely accepting eternal extinction and nonbeing, or excitedly moving on to a new reincarnation, to an immortality of the disembodied soul, or a paradisaical state of blissful continuity. In any case, the message is heard: death is not so bad; it may just be better than life. As the writer on religions, Alan Watts, declared in a recorded address, broadcast posthumously, "Death should be welcomed with rejoicing. . . . We might form an Institute of Creative Dying." (So Koheleth now speaks the same words as in the time of ancient Israel, but in a cheerful rather than melancholy mood.) But if death is indeed so enjoyable and desirable, or just a gentle passing on, we wonder why Kübler-Ross has had to deal so extensively with experiences of fear, shock, outrage, and grief among those who are dying.

Morbidity of mood is the dark twin of light frivolity. It is the cobra-eye of death, attracting, entrancing, compelling the devotee to hold still and passively receive the fatal bite. It may take the form of romantic reflection on *ein Liebestod*, when the archetypical connection between love and death is enacted by Tristan, heroically, with Isolde, or Romeo, sadly, with Juliet. Or else the morbid dwelling upon death tempts one to thoughts of suicide, when death seems the better option for the young person who is just weary of it all or for the older person afraid of terminal pain.

It is this dual attitude toward death that has become so much a fad since the 1960s, as it both feeds on a devalued sense of life and contributes to the further debasement of life. It is time to call "Enough!" Thanatology is unquestionably a serious discipline; pondering the meaning of death by scientific, philosophical, and theological methods continues to be needed. Not at all needed, however, are the vulgarized side effects that only distract minds from the existential tragedy of death and serve to minimize the intrinsic worth of human life. To make the "grim reaper" of the *Totentanz*, the medieval dance of death, appear as a smiling friend is a gross deception. To believe that a subconscious "death wish" potentially dominates everyone's behavior, or that Martin Heidegger's concept of "being-unto-death" is the annulment of the goodness of human existence, is a view to be challenged, unmasked, and overcome. To combine such thought with a romantic aspiring after nirvana, as some do, is to invert the long-held Jewish and Christian belief that life is the nearly absolute good, while death is the "last enemy" to be overcome by God's redemptive action in history.

DEBASEMENT OF LIFE AND DESTRUCTION OF HOPE

Three interrelated expressions of the debasement of human life in the present time thus appear before us who live in the Euro-American culture. One is the sheer wastage of human life and its resources, whether intentionally or inadvertently, by direct human agency or other forces. The second is the generally evident callousness toward human life, whether due to a culturally conditioned indifference or to a cynical rejection of all that is thought to be good in life. The third dimension is the vulgarized, frivolous or morbid embracing of death as the last and best benefit in mortal existence.

Most national cultures have experienced the first of these, and many in past and present in greater or lesser degree have expressed the second. Americans have no peculiar claim on wastage and callousness. Indeed, as has been suggested, the preponderance of sentiment in the nineteenth and twentieth centuries, if not earlier, has favored the care and protection of life. But American society's recent infatuation with the problems of death and even with the desirability of death is a new experience, a discovery of unrivaled scope and insidious consequences.

How do prodigality, callousness, and frivolity-morbidity serve to debase life? Chiefly, by destroying hope. Human beings hope. Animals only survive. Merely to survive as a species satisfies the animals. Merely to survive as individuals or a species cannot satisfy humanity. This is a definitive distinction.

If it can be agreed that this distinction is not only categorical but also of primary significance, then it follows that human life without hope for fulfillment is debased. Even the debased life is human and always valued, whether this dereliction from normalcy is due to extreme physical and mental disability, deprivation of conditions and goods needed for development of potentials, or to some form of moral depravity. But without hope in this temporal existence and beyond it, there can be no enhancement of life. "Where there's life there's hope," says the old Latin motto *Ubi vita, ibi spes.* But the formula is reciprocal, and the converse has the deeper meaning: where there is hope there is life.

2

LIFE,
THE GREAT PRESUPPOSITION
STILL UNDEFINED

THE NEED FOR A CONCEPT OF LIFE

Some things are taken for granted. Everyone knows what they are. They require no intellectual definition. In any case, the definition falls short of the experienced reality. It seems that love is such a reality; so are beauty, ugliness, and evil. Also life. Who does not know what "life" means? It is self-evident to all. We can say, "To have life is to be alive." I know what life is because I live, people live, animals live; plants, cells, and viruses live. There is something that distinguishes these from everything else which is inert and dead. And that is life. Why ask any more?

Common sense thinking often contains wisdom. But common thoughts such as those mentioned above do not define life. They only point to it as an experienced and perceived phenomenon. Life is not defined simply by saying that it means being alive. That is like saying that motion is the property of whatever moves—hardly a helpful definition.

In much speaking and writing about questions of life today this common acceptance of self-evident meaning is presupposed. The discussion may be philosophical or religious, scientific or ethical, argumentative or polemical, intellectual or commonplace—in all cases it is usually assumed that people know what life means. But do they?

Doubts about the understanding of life are not entertained by people who "accept the world the way it is" and do not sense either need or disposition to be bothered by scientific, philosophical, or theological debates. After all, they say, life is something every person possesses in virtue of existing. It is that without which you are dead. Beyond human reference and in the broadest terms, life is that strange, universal power that enables matter to move itself, to reproduce its own kind, and to undergo evolutionary changes, or mutations, of a genetic character. In narrower, human terms, life is the animating principle that is somehow integrated with the biological physical organism to constitute a developing or actualized sentient, self-conscious person. Since the source of this latter dimension of human life, namely, self-consciousness, cannot be discovered, seen, demonstrated, or proved, it can be proposed as a matter of religious belief, conventional wisdom, or conjecture. So even here, in the realm of ordinary, unsophisticated common-sense thinking about life, the most profound and perplexing questions about life confront each person.

Our colloquial speech reveals the difficulty of defining "life." Like many words in all languages, it is ambiguous. Used as a noun, it can have several meanings:

- Origin of life (biology)
- Life of Gandhi (biography)
- Common life (social existence)
- Private life (individual existence)
- Life of the party: *la dolce vita* (vivacity)
- True to life (phenomena)
- Value of life (significance, meaning)
- Eternal life (fulfillment)

"Life" is also an adjective, conveying other nuances:

- Life insurance (monetary value)
- Life member (duration)
- Life sciences (living matter)

If we are discussing the tragedies of life, or life among the Eskimos, or the pro-life movement, or the purpose and mystery of life, which of the possible meanings do we have in mind? Confusion clouds communication in discussions and debates, especially those of a gravely serious nature, for lack of a single definition. Because it is not self-evident in all cases, it may be wiser to recognize that there is no common presupposition but rather an open question.

Depending upon the context, the word "life" may refer narrowly, on one extreme, to the most simple forms of organic material at molecular and cellular levels. Talk about the "origin of life" often means no more than a question of how it happens that these tiny bodies are able to reproduce themselves and manifest mutations in their progeny. "Is there life on Mars?" is a question about the capability of Martian chemistry to produce and sustain the simplest forms of organic matter. On the opposite extreme from such simplicity of meaning, "life" is an omnibus term that conveys references to the whole range of organic life as well as the fullness of intellectual and spiritual attainment of human beings. Between these extremes are many varieties and calibrations of meaning of this vital monosyllable. It is no wonder that the writer of the article in *Encyclopaedia Britannica* expressed despair over "life" by calling it "a phenomenon almost impossible to define or to explain in all its varying aspects."[1]

If any inquiry into the phenomenon of life is to be intelligible as well as useful, some major distinctions are required. These may fall logically into three categories with some further refinements within each. We shall here speak of the three in turn: description, analysis, and evaluation.

Any living thing which can be seen by human eyes can be described in numerous ways: in terms of its externally observed appearance, shape, dimensions, color, texture, appendages; also in terms of its life cycle, growth pattern, characteristic behavior, and customary habitat. Vast quantities of literature, drawings, and photographs have been created and catalogued over many centuries; and they are the descriptive legacies for all humanity, left by an immense population of botanists, biologists, and zoologists of many specialized branches. They show us the incalculable range of organic life in all orders of complexity—individual specimens, species, genera, orders, classes, and phyla in the great taxonomic schema of classification. Biologists are unsure of the approximate numbers of different species of organisms. The estimates actually run between five million and ten million, numbers which no mind can really conceive. As with snowflakes, no two specimens are exactly alike. Yet, whatever the extant number of species, these are probably less than one percent of all that have ever existed on earth. This is why the rueful assertion of worried ecologists, that hundreds of species are becoming extinct each day, is a credible one, despite one's initial disbelief of the claim. As a team of leading biologists agreed, "The totality of biological diversity is almost incomprehensible to the human imagination."[2] Undaunted by the inexhaustible numbers, the experts keep describing the life forms they see, from unicellular protoplasm with its so-called package of genes to plants and animals of increasing organic complexity and size, and on to sentient animals and human beings. All have life; all are alive. To say the word "life" is to comprehend them all. But the particular descriptions say nothing of the source of life nor the value of it.

The need for defining and refining a concept of life in general and human life in particular becomes more insistent with each new wave of biological research, with each advance in our knowledge of ecological interdependence of flora and fauna, and with the rapidly developing techniques by which genetic structures can be modified at will and human bodies can be aided in forestalling the cessation of life. The analytic approach to life requires the research of many specialized sciences within the biological field: microbiology and genetics, biochemistry, biophysics, neurology, evolutionary and developmental biology. Such sciences seek through the most exacting and patient research to find explanations for such problems as the causes and sequences of organic life, the power of growth and the differentiation of cells, the coordinated movement or function of every part of the organism, the microsecond responses of nerve cells to sensory stimuli, and the directing power of the brain. Analysis requires more of the scientist-observer than simply the ability to see and describe. It requires as well a mental capacity for acute perception, reflection, imagination, and definition. This is because an ultimate question is always pressing upon the analyst. That is the tantalizing, nagging question, What causes life? By what originating, driving power and process do irreducible forms of living matter divide and replicate themselves? How are they instructed by certain combinations of thousands of genes, which are themselves com-

30

posed of nucleic acids, to become the muscle tissue of a termite rather than the sex organ of a bee, the eye of a potato rather than the eyebrow of a girl, the purple petal of an iris rather than the feather of a cockatoo? Can the secret ever be known by microbiological analysis? Or must that ever be a philosophical matter?

Even if scientists, artists, and photographers could produce descriptions of all the millions of species, and even if scientists joined by philosophers and theologians could agree on the analysis and identifying of life's cause or causes, there would still be no necessary basis for ascribing relative values to all the living forms. If there are moral considerations or laws based upon the intrinsic worth of whatever lives, do they apply to the vegetable as well as the animal kingdom, to the nonsentient as well as the self-conscious? Or are these codes of value just the convenient inventions and constructs of human imagination? We learn more and more of ecological systems, recognizing the delicate balances of plant and animal life under specific conditions of moisture and climate. We discern a continuum of dependency for both food and reproduction among bacteria, plants, worms, insects, fish, birds, reptiles, and mammals. Within the continuum of the food cycles and reproductive processes are the necessary interactions of pure elements and chemical compounds, effected by electrical charges of their atoms—all of which can be described by scientific symbols and vivid prose.

Why is it of any importance to the cosmic order, though, or even to this terrestrial sphere that these cycles of survival keep going? Flowers, insects, fish, and birds develop protective coloration and strategies. Why? Many animals defend their young, some their kin, and a few protect other species. Why? Living organisms kill and eat other organisms, and some eat their own species or offspring. Human beings also kill with prodigality. They kill not only for food, or in defense, but for reasons of sport or greed or hatred, or for no good reason at all. Where in all this killing and eating are the precious lodes of intrinsic value of life found? And how, within the limits of the species Homo sapiens, are values—both relative and absolute—attached to human lives in differing conditions and stages of development: the embryo, fetus, infant; the physically deformed and mentally impaired child lacking capacity for so-called meaningful life; the morally degenerate, the normally healthy and well-behaved, the unconscious and comatose ones, or those persons who are in the process of dying?

VITALISM vs. MECHANISM

Whether life is being described, analyzed, or evaluated, the irreducible factor is the power of vitality itself. In conventional language we often speak of "the miracle of life." This is a misnomer, even though the phenomena of life are indeed awe-inspiring. A miracle is an absolutely extraordinary happening: unique in character as well as time. Once a miracle has been repeated, it becomes ordinary. Each manifestation of vitality, however astonishing to see and contemplate, is not literally a miracle. Some facts may seem to be miraculous: the fact that within an acorn, barely two centimeters in length, there is the potential oak tree; that a twenty-meter whale begins to exist as a pair of conjoined germ cells; or that Leonardo da Vinci was at first an embryo too small to be seen. Despite their wonder, these and thousands of other illustrations of living phenomena which our eyes behold and our minds record are, in virtue of their naturalness, constantly being repeated and are fairly predictable. They are not entitled to be called miracles. They are facts of life. But their full facticity remains for us a mystery.

Each child today who achieves the reflective capacity of, say, a seven-year-old thinks at least occasionally about the meaning of being alive. We may also assume that our remotest ancestors pondered the same question. Art and religion, poetry and philosophy were always the media by which the tentative, groping answers to the question were communicated. What is life? Why is there life? What is not-life, or death?

In the literate cultures of antiquity two kinds of answers were framed out of observation, experience, and reflection. One asserted that the only reality is what exists physically and materially. Therefore, life itself must have arisen somehow from physical matter. The other answer held that all living things and beings, while physically material in substance or body, are vivified or animated by a power of life external to matter. The first was the answer of mechanistic materialism, the second the answer of vitalism. These two general categories of thought have constituted the point-counterpoint of theoretical tension since ancient times. Just where, when, how, and by whom they were first conceived and expressed we cannot know. We do have literature to show that various particular ways of conceiving of matter and immaterial vitality have fluctuated during more than two-and-one-half millennia. And even today the two general types of theory remain as alternative possibilities of understanding life.

Theories they are; but their importance is not merely theoretical. It is not solely for the satisfaction of our hunger for knowledge that we seek enlightenment about life's nature. That appetite for curiosity is indeed compelling. It provides the impetus for philosophers and scientists and other persons who are literally thoughtful. Beyond knowledge as such, however, are its great implications for human self-understanding, religion, morality, and social structures of agreeable goodness. The ways by which we human beings conceive of life have always affected our modes of valuing or disregarding it, enhancing or debasing it, protecting or destroying it.

The Perennial Vitality of Vitalism

The vitalistic theory had preeminence in primal cultures, according to the thesis of Hans Jonas, a much-respected philosopher of biology. Many evidences drawn from archaeology and earliest writings indicate that the initial outlook of humanity's awakening intelligence was one of what Jonas calls monistic pan-vitalism or pan-psychism.[3] Their view was monistic in the sense that physical matter and mind or spirit or soul was indissoluble; no dualistic disjunction was perceived to separate them. They were pan-vitalistic because literally all things were believed to be kept alive by a vital force. Men and women lived uncritically in the "climate of a universal ontology of life," writes Jonas. It was sensed as "the original ontological dominance of life."[4]

Early philosophies and religious beliefs, as recalled in art and ritual, testified to this intuitive understanding. Not only the myriad plants and animals, but the inorganic things of nature as well, were thought to be alive. The ceaseless movements of rivers, ocean tides and currents, skyborne clouds; the fierce power of winds which uprooted great trees and moved the sand dunes; the tremors of the earth and the fiery expectorations of volcanic mountains; rockslides and snowslides—all the world seemed restlessly mobile, driven by awesome powers of change, threatening human survival. The distinction between life and motion was so unclear that, as language was being shaped, the two concepts were related in choosing words for life: to live was to be automobile, self-moving. Moreover, the universal attitude of animism made it acceptable to attribute some kind of soul-force or vitality even to immobile objects such as natural rock formations, man-carved pillars of stone or wooden statues.

Awareness of the pervasiveness of living things throughout the terrestrial environment is not an experience limited to naive, culturally primitive people. Artists, poets, philosophers, and scientists also know the irrepressible impulses of living matter. The German philosopher of both nature and politics Johann Gottlieb Fichte envisaged in the year 1800 what the world is truly like:

> The dead burdensome mass which merely filled space has disappeared, and instead the eternal river of life, energy and act rushes and roars along—the river of original life, of thy life, thou Infinite. . . . I am akin to thee, and what I see around me is akin to myself; everything is animated and ensouled and looks at me with the translucent eyes of the spirit, and addresses my heart in spiritual harmonies.[5]

A more concrete experience of his identity with the totality of life gave to the famous organist-theologian-medical missionary Albert Schweitzer his doctrine of *Ehrfurcht vor dem Leben.* His German phrase emphasizes more powerfully than "reverence for life" what a sense of awe he felt in the presence of all living beings and things.

It was not by meticulous empirical observation as a naturalist that he formulated this all-embracing concept, nor by the study of books on botany and zoology, nor simply by appropriating the do-no-harm doctrine of the Jain sect of Hinduism. This overpowering awareness seized Schweitzer with the force of a revelation while he was taking a one-hundred-sixty-mile boat trip up the Ogowe River from Cape Lopez in central Africa one day in September 1915.[6] It was as though he moved through an atmosphere saturated with vitality: the herd of hippopotamuses and the scaly creatures of the water; fibrous growths of the fecund soil; grasses, vines, ferns, and towering trees; slithering reptiles, frenetic monkeys, crashing boars; countless insects and birds filling the air with humming vibrations and feathery flashes; and everywhere beside, below, around, and within him the unicellular bacteria, germs, and nearly invisible particles of reproducing matter. It was for Schweitzer a moment of revelation and realization, that all this immensity of life required his humble reverence, his fearful respect, and his avowal to avoid as much as possible the killing of life. All of ethics, for Schweitzer, must thus be determined by respect and awe for the marvelous phenomenon of life. Life's worthiness of respect derives from what he styled "the infinite, inexplicable, forward-urging will in which all Being is grounded."[7] For him, however, this power of life is not identified with the Creator-God of the Bible.

The sensitive thinkers of ancient India reflected intensely upon life. And Schweitzer's expressions about his attitude toward life are reminiscent of their concepts. The ancient Hindus gave Sanskrit words to two related concepts: *prāna* and *ahimsā*. The universal principle of vitality was called *prāna*, the Life Force itself. Like *ruah* in Hebrew and *pneuma* in Greek, *prāna* is a word derived from the experience of breathing air and feeling the wind. Animals having pulmonary systems, however simple or complex, share the same characteristic of being dependent upon *prāna* for living. Thus the ancient discipline of *yoga*, intended for both mental meditation and bodily health, requires proper breathing. It is of fundamental importance for the inspiring of the Life Force. So *atman*, the soul, is borne by *prāna*. Parents continue to live in their children by *prāna*. But what is its source? While Hebrew religious belief was developing the thought that Yahweh the Creator is the source of the breath of life, the Hindu mind located the source of *prāna* in the sun. This was actually an early anticipation of the conclusive findings by modern science about photosynthesis and other products of solar energy. All life depends to large extent upon the sun, even though the sun is not the original source of life.

Prominence was given to the concept of *ahimsā* by adherents of Jainism, who even today look back to Mahavira, a contemporary of Gautama Buddha, as their teacher. *Ahimsā* expresses respect for all that lives and the "renunciation of the will to kill and to damage."[8] Although *ahimsā* has come to connote compassion and harmlessness toward life, it was originally grounded in an absolutely ascetic desire to avoid defilement in the world so that one's soul, or *jiva*, could enjoy release. Even inadvertent, unintentional killing of life was thought to damage and scar the personal perfection of the seeker. Jains, therefore, would not engage in agriculture because digging in the earth inevitably hurts or kills animal life. And the Jain priest today wears a gauze mask and sweeps his path with a small broom as he walks, lest unseen life be killed by inhalation or by crushing under foot. While conceding the practical impossibility of fulfilling *ahimsā* in all actions of one's life, Albert Schweitzer still called its development into a religious and moral philosophy "one of the greatest events in the spiritual history of mankind."[9] It was a decisive move from mere primordial feeling of awe at the spectacle of life to an attribution of intrinsic value in all of life.

Almost contemporary with the development of such life concepts in India, that is, about the fourth century B.C., the great Greek philosopher-scientist Aristotle pondered similar thoughts about the power of vitality. So far as we know, there was no other person of the ancient world who made such comprehensive studies of numerous forms of organic life. His prodigious descriptions of animal behavior and reproduction were augmented by the reported results of careful dissection and his postulated theories concerning the why and how of living organisms. Needing to have a workable idea of the potency of life, Aristotle proposed a hypothesis and gave it a name: *entelecheia*. He coined the word from the root idea of *telos*, meaning purpose or goal, and the verb *echein*, to have. The entelechy is the force that possesses purpose and drives living matter and organisms to their fulfillment of *telos*. It is not a single, uniform power of life nor a power of cosmic purpose;[10] but it manifests itself variously in ways that are appropriate to the many diverse living beings. It may appear as the "vital fire" within male semen. Or it may be expressed as the soul, *psuchē*, which in turn exists in differing ways or dimensions, the finest of which is the human exercise of reason.

If India and Greece were the lands in which the most sophisticated philosophical formulations of pan-vitalistic thought were devised, they shared with others in Africa and Asia the various inchoate convictions that an energizing force of indeterminate source and nature was the cause and sustaining support of all life.

Materialism: Living Matter or Material Life?

In view of the prevailing acceptance of pan-vitalism it is really amazing that some persons had both the originality of thought and the intellectual courage to challenge what almost everyone believed about the source of life. Yet certain notable philosophers, in Greece especially, reasoned that the basis of all reality is matter as such, rather than life-energy, soul, spirit, or eternal mind. Their names are linked together in textbooks of philosophy: Parmenides, Zeno, Anaxagoras, Empedocles, Leucippus, Democritus, Epicurus, and, later on, Lucretius of Rome. From the sixth century B.C. to the first they propounded their materialistic theories about the constitutive atoms to be found in all things, whether inert or living. They did not deny the reality of the human soul, but believed it to be constituted of "exceedingly minute bodies" or "very small seeds," as Lucretius called the atoms.[11] It also seemed natural, therefore, that maggots, flies, and worms simply arose from the decaying, putrid organic waste. This idea, known as "hylozoism," literally "matter-life," persisted late into history, until it was disproved first by Francesco Redi in 1668 and Louis Pasteur in 1860.

The ancient materialists argued with zest in favor of their explanations of natural phenomena in terms of matter moving at random rather than of any immaterial or metaphysical power directing all things toward completion. They were pitted against the formidable opposition of the two great philosophers Plato and Aristotle, both of whom, despite their sharply differing accounts of the spiritual or soulish realities, insisted that the power of all organic life and the capacity of humans to enjoy living were derived from sources beyond the mundane and temporal stuff of the world. Being unaware of the stark limitations on their capacity for scientific investigation, they relied inevitably upon intuitive and imaginative thought rather than empirical and experimental analysis. These materialists showed ingenious and prodigious ability to perceive and postulate the atomistic and mechanistic notions of physics and biology. In this they were two thousand years ahead of the harbingers of the era of modern science.

Materialism, however, in ancient times was an exception to the prevailing views. Museums are crammed with archaeological evidences of the early awareness of the vital powers which generated and perpetuated all things. Some were monistic, equating spirit and matter. Others were dualistic, holding spirit and matter in tension. Whether spiritually good or demonically evil, the powers controlled all life and the order of nature. The reality of life was readily accepted as fact rather than mystery. The problem for human understanding was not the "mystery of life," then, but rather the mystery of death and its consequences. According to Hans Jonas, again, the ancient peoples' obvious devotion to the appurtenances of death—rituals, prayers, burial practices, sarcophagi, and tombs—did not express either an acceptance or an exaltation of death. It was, instead, their protest against the "outrage which the fact of mortality inflicts on panvitalistic conviction."[12] It was natural and normal and good for everything to be alive. Death was the unnatural, abnormal contradiction of all perceived reality.

Painting the canvas of religious and philosophical history with broad strokes, Jonas shows how the total reversal of this attitude toward life and death was effected in European culture by the rise of an empirical, scientific method and materialistic world view after the sixteenth century. "Vitalistic monism is replaced by mechanistic monism," he writes.[13] Lifeless, inert matter came quickly to be seen as the normal state of nature. The problem posed by the new science was no longer, How can it be that living things die? but instead, How can life arise from a world of nonliving material? "But the possibility of a living matter is quite inconceivable," wrote Immanuel Kant in *The Critique of Teleological Judgement.*

> The very conception of it involves self-contradiction, since lifelessness, *inertia*, constitutes the essential characteristic of matter. . . . Its possibility can in no way be perceived *a priori.* Hence there must be a vicious circle in the explanation, if the finality of nature in organized beings is sought to be derived from the life of matter and if this life in turn is only to be known in organized beings, so that no conception of its possibility can be formed apart from such an experience. Hence hylozoism does not perform what it promises.[14]

Now, five centuries after the beginning of modern science and two centuries after Kant, the question of life's arising from matter is not only asked in a serious way; it is partially answered by biophysicists and microbiologists. "Today we strive to explain the animate in terms of the inanimate," wrote the English biologist C. U. M. Smith. "Twenty-five hundred years ago the problem simply did not exist."[15]

Certainly the balance shifted in European thought from theories of vitalism to those of materialism between the intellectual decline of ancient Athens and the ascendancy of Renaissance Florence, Paris, Amsterdam, and London. In their fine discussions of this momentous change, both Jonas and Smith fail to give due emphasis to the influence of Christianity upon natural philosophy. Penetrating the Graeco-Roman culture of the first to the fourth centuries A.D., Christian theology did two things. First, it brought to Gentile civilization the Hebraic understanding of human life. This was the nondualistic conception of life as the personal integration of soul and body, both being created by God and both as a unity of highest, indispensable value. The belief so expressed in the Hebrew Bible and invariably accepted by most Christians was quite different from the views inherited from classic Greece, whether the materialisms of Democritus and Epicurus or the vitalisms of Plato and Aristotle. The biblical doctrine asserted that the one, eternal, and transcendent God created humanity—and each individual person within humanity—with a deliberate purpose. Likewise, God's creative power brought all living things into existence in a world environment where the divine, providential power enables all life to perpetuate itself. The clear inference of this idea of divine creation was that it happened, and still happens, *ex nihilo*, out of nothing. This equally contradicted the materialists' atomistic theories, the Platonic concept of eternal forms, the Stoics' version of the fire of reason, and the Aristotelian theory of an Unmoved Prime Mover and a necessitarian purpose to things and beings.[16] Apparently, Christian faith and practice, as legitimized by the Emperor Constantine in the fourth century and propagated throughout the declining empire, should have displaced all the inherited philosophies of life which originated in the *age d'or* of Greece. But it did not displace them; it modified them.

Christianity's second effect was to enter into philosophical alliances with the two main streams of Hellenic thought that were totally alien and opposed to materialism. The biblical ideas of God and of faith in Jesus Christ were, in a restricted sense, very materialistic. This means that God created all matter and called it "good." Creation is good, not morally, but because it is appropriate for his purposes. It also means that the supreme disclosure of God's will in Jesus Christ was done in a material way—by becoming flesh, incarnation. Yet, neither of these affirmations of created matter could be reconciled to the materialism of the Greek philosophers, much less identified with it. So it was only to the Greek traditions of the goodness of the immortal soul that Christian thinkers were drawn—to the "new Platonism" taught by two famous Egyptians, Philo of the first century and Plotinus of the third; and also to the Aristotelianism rediscovered, reinterpreted, and "baptized" by Thomas Aquinas and Western Catholicism in the thirteenth century. Just as Paul had lectured on the Athenian Acropolis to Stoic and Epicurean philosophers and told them the true name of the "unknown god" that they acknowledged, so Christian philosophers gave a name and identity to the entelechy of Aristotle and the eternal soul of Plato: it was the name of the God and Father of Jesus Christ, active in creating and sustaining all life by his immanent Holy Spirit.

Without conforming to the very much differing philosophies of Plato and Aristotle, therefore, a new kind of Christian vitalism arose; and it exercised a dominating influence upon both intellectual inquiry and popular piety in Europe for some fourteen centuries.

Two thousand years make a long bridge of time between Aristotle and the one man who most nearly emulated his philosophical achievement. This was the German genius, Immanuel Kant. Like the great Greek, Kant also attempted to bring virtually the totality of human experience and science within the range of his own comprehensive thought. In 1790, he published the third of his famous critiques, *The Critique of Teleological Judgement*. The book is his astute analysis of the state of the biological sciences and of philosophical efforts to explicate the source, power and purpose of life. From his study in Königsberg, East Prussia, Kant looked back upon, and evaluated, more than two centuries of vigorous intellectual awakening and ferment of debate about life. And he died at the opening of the nineteenth century, when discoveries about life were being made with accelerating frequency and importance.

Studies of life were still secondary to the mathematical and physical sciences, however. The main thrust of the rebirth of "natural philosophy" and scientific investigation was achieved in the fields of mathematics, geometry, astronomy, and physics. As the greatest minds of the era—those of Copernicus, Kepler, Francis Bacon, Descartes, Galileo, and Newton—revealed the secrets of the structure and motion of the earth and the planetary system, it is not so strange that their projected views of animal life and the human species were primarily physical and mechanistic. Conceptions of life were derived largely from material considerations peculiar to the physical sciences.

The human body had been obscured for more than a thousand years by the modesty, prudishness, and otherworldliness that the church's teachings imposed upon European social customs. In the fifteenth and sixteenth centuries the body was disrobed and explored by artists and anatomists. Inspired by the rediscovered Greek sculpture, artists of the Renaissance perfected their knowledge of physiology, both human and animal. Leonardo da Vinci's eyes seemed almost to penetrate physical structure; and his hand traced the lines of bone, muscle, flesh, skin, and hair with an accuracy that has never been surpassed. He and Michelangelo and other great artists dissected cadavers, and in so doing helped indirectly such scientists as Vesalius, the anatomist, and William Harvey, the cardiologist, achieve their discoveries of the workings of the human machine. The word "machine" is used deliberately because this was how all living organisms came increasingly to be known. In his *Discourse on the Method of Rightly Conducting the Reason* (1637), René Descartes wrote that he found little or no difference between the functioning of animal and human bodies, both flesh and blood. As living bodies they are kept alive by what he arbitrarily called "animal spirits" and "subtle fluids." "This will not seem strange," he observed, "to those, who, knowing how many different *automata* or moving machines can be made by the industry of man, without employing in so doing more than a very few parts in comparison with the great multitude of bones, muscles, nerves, arteries, veins or other parts that are found in the body of each animal. From this aspect," he concluded, "the body is regarded as a machine which, having been made by the hands of God, is incomparably better arranged . . . than any of those which can be invented by man."[17] What makes the human machine different from all animals, of course, is the rational soul, the power to think, that determines the very being of a person. For Descartes, to think is to be.

While it is only fair to hold up Descartes' idea of the biological machine as the representative concept of his era, it would be less than accurate to class him among the thoroughgoing materialists. After all, he continually struggled to maintain his Catholic Christian faith in the context of a threatening rationalism. So he did not abandon belief in God as both the maker of these animal machines and the dispenser of the rational soul to the humans among them. While claiming that the soul should be "joined and united" so closely to the body that it may thus "form a true man," Descartes still subscribed to a dualistic anthropology; for, he added, "our soul is in its nature entirely independent of body [and] . . . is not liable to die with it."[18]

It may not be unfair or disrespectful to the religious temperament of some seventeenth-century scientists to judge that their professed religion was a residual faith that diminished as the years passed. The Christian belief in God as Creator and Governor, as well as the Platonized idea of the immortal soul as the temporary inhabitant, so to speak, of the mortal, mechanical body were at this time still modifying and mitigating the inclination of these men toward materialism. But leading thinkers of the eighteenth century felt fewer inhibitions about discarding the supernatural, supersensible factors that had so long been employed to explain the inexplicable aspects of human life. It was the century of Enlightenment, empiricism, rationalism, skepticism, and, for some thinkers, complete materialism. Notable among these was the French physician, Julien Offray de la Mettrie, whose main book is remembered more for its representative title than its contents: *L'homme machine (Man the Machine)*. For him, the mechanical model of all organic life, humans included, needed no dualistic qualification. No one can argue against the observed fact that living bodies are made of matter, which is subject to chemical analysis; nor can the similarities of levers, fulcra, pumps, and valves to muscles, bones, arteries, heart, and lungs be denied.

The popularity of this way of thinking about the human organism is illustrated by an extract from the sermon of the eighteenth century's leading preacher John Wesley, who fancied himself an amateur scientist as well:

> How fearfully and wonderfully wrought into innumerable fibres, nerves, membranes, muscles, arteries, veins, vessels of various kinds! And how amazingly is the dust connected with water, with inclosed [sic], circulating fluids, diversified a thousand ways by a thousand tubes and strainers. Yea, and how wonderfully is air impacted into every part, solid or fluid, of the animal machine. . . . But all this would not avail, were not ethereal fire intimately mixed both with this earth, air and water. And all these elements are mingled together in the most exact proportions.[19]

Ominous as the word "mechanism" may sound to one who defends the self-transcending reality of the mind and the singular virtue of each soul, biological investigation and description by the eighteenth century had shown what the burgeoning life sciences of the nineteenth and twentieth have made conclusive. Thus Kant decreed: "We may and should explain all products and events of nature, even the most purposive, so far as in our power lies, on mechanical lines."[20]

Nevertheless, Kant was wholly dissatisfied with the previous efforts of mechanistic materialists to conclude their conception of life so abruptly. What he missed in mechanism was the quality that Aristotle had sought by contemplative reason and what Christian philosophers affirmed ultimately as a matter of faith, namely purpose, finality. In all of nature Kant discerned a direction toward ends, a teleological impulsion. As he wrote, "when teleology is applied to physics, we speak with perfect justice of the wisdom, the economy, the forethought, the beneficence of nature."[21] If this is so for nonliving matter, how much more is it for the living? What source of power gives this purposeful direction to all matter? Since the centuries of Graeco-Roman grandeur and glory, the power had been attributed to hylozoism. But Kant rejected this, as we noted above, because it was inconceivable. Moreover, it simply begs the question by giving an artificial name to a mystery. Still in the writing of the great Kant, then, the problem remains: mechanical structure, yes; materialism, no.

Kant's Christian beliefs were explicit enough. But he would not take the easy path of his family's Lutheran pietism to resolve the problem of ends in a nonscientific way. He conceded that theism had the advantage over materialism: "by attributing intelligence to the original Being" it accounts for order in nature, self-conscious intelligence and freedom in humans, and hence a purposeful *telos* for all creation. But this perspective belongs to faith rather than to sight, to the reflective judgment rather than to the determinant judgment that philosophy and science require.

When Kant rejected theistic teleology as the solution of the problem of life, however, he did not mean that he denied the possibility of its being true. We can conceive the purposive ends, even though we are quite incapable of demonstrating or verifying them. We are therefore justified, wrote Kant, "to consider nature, and thus life itself, according to both 'mechanical laws' and teleological laws . . . without being disturbed by the apparent conflict that arises between principles."[22] Both are real, but their reality is apprehended in differing ways. To borrow and paraphrase Kant's most famous dictum (words engraved on his tomb): the most awe-inspiring things known as "the starry heavens," are subject, as are living organisms, to mechanical laws; and "the moral law within," manifests, like human reason and personal freedom, the finality of purposeful ends.

Materialistic mechanism or vitalistic power: which makes organic life possible? Or is there, perhaps, in addition a soul-force that operates only in human beings, while all other kinds of life are only of physical and chemical nature?

Immanuel Kant died as the nineteenth century began. He thus lived near the midpoint of the era of modern science, between its origin and the present day. Considering the scope, depth, and ingenuity of his philosophical system, he and his devotees may have felt confident that the competition of vitalism and mechanism had been resolved by his dialectical scheme. Both the mechanical functioning of the organism, as scientifically described, and teleological direction of life, as postulated, were affirmed. Only their modes of being perceived were of differing orders. Kant's synthesis seemed to make sense as the way to accommodate both biological science and the dominating idealistic philosophy of Europe. It was thus appropriated by a succession of the most notable thinkers of the nineteenth-century Romantic Movement: philosophers, mainly German, such as Johann Gottlieb Fichte, Georg Wilhelm Friedrich Hegel, Friedrich Schelling, Arthur Schopenhauer, and Friedrich Nietzsche; poets, British and German, such as Samuel T. Coleridge, William Wordsworth, and Johann Wolfgang von Goethe; and following in their train, theologians such as Friedrich Schleiermacher. These were the eminent molders of intellectual positions from which appraisals of scientific advance were made. The debate between advocates of vitalism and mechanism continued with vigor and passion throughout this eventful century.[23]

Biologists, however, in concert with chemists and physicists, were pressing their research into the nature of matter, and were being pressed by their findings to intensify and solidify their commitment to the theory of a physicochemical basis of life. One by one, as the technology of the laboratory and especially of the microscope improved, the ingredients of matter, both inert and organic, became known. John Dalton described in 1803 the atomic basis of the chemistry of gases, liquids, and solids. The unknown key to the understanding of organic molecular structure was found twenty-five years later when Friedrich Wöhler in Germany synthesized urea. This landmark achievement has often been noted as a refutation of vitalism, although it is doubtful that Wöhler so regarded it. Even so, his Swedish teacher, Jöns Jacob Berzelius, and his contemporary, Justus Liebig, both held to the presence of a vital force.

The universal presence of cells, first suggested in 1665 by Robert Hooke, was demonstrated in 1858 by Rudolf Virchow, showing that living cells are always derived from preceding ones. By 1866, the patient, perceptive monk, Gregor Johann Mendel, had found the primary principle of genetic inheritance, even though he did not know the identity of the as yet unnamed genes, which came to light some thirty years later. However, in 1873 those composite genetic determinants, which in 1888 were first called chromosomes, were examined and partly understood. In the time scale of the late twentieth century, scientific advances move so rapidly that the chain of discoveries in the nineteenth seems slow by comparison. However, in the whole frame of modern science the accelerating pace of decisive achievements was indeed rapid.

Rapidly diminishing at the same time was the apparent force of argument in favor of the vitalistic and teleological concepts of life. Most distressing to the people of Christian and Judaic persuasion, as well as to many humanists, was the mounting evidence that human life is not so one-sidedly different from other forms of animal life as had long been believed on the bases of either the Bible or Aristotelian philosophy. Is not humanity the "crown of creation"? Is it not earth's highest link, the veritable jeweled clasp, in "the great chain of being"? How could these self-evident notions survive the accumulating evidence found by the scientists, who dug up and reassembled prehistoric bones and fossil remains, who penetrated the structure and substance of molecules and cells, or described at last the ponderous evidence for the origin of species and the evolution of all living things through the natural selection of those capable of surviving?

The decisive, yet incomplete, theories of Charles Darwin and Alfred Russel Wallace were announced in 1858 and published in 1859. They suddenly provided a new context for the perennial debate over life's origin and nature. This was new on at least three counts. First, the debate became fully public, rather than being confined to scientists and philosophers. Second, it directly engaged the institutions of churches and academic theology, which rested firmly (so it was believed) on the infallible text of the Bible. Third, in the scientific area itself Darwinism realigned the sides that were contending about chance, necessity, and teleology.

In the public context, agitation over the explosive impact of evolution was understandable and predictable. The stability of creation seemed to be shaken. The dignity of humanity was debased by the popularized caricature of Darwin's *The Descent of Man*: the idea that we are "descended from monkeys" was an insult to all human beings.

The challenge to Christian religious teaching was probably more devastating than Darwin expected (and today, more than a century later, the implications of this challenge continue to be contested). In Darwin's time, the historical-critical interpretation of the Bible was just a novel and dangerously radical experiment. Most Christians believed that what was written must be accepted literally because it was dictated by God. Thus, special creation of each and every species was implied by the Genesis story. And there were two actual persons named Adam and Eve, created in full maturity, who were the first ancestors of all people. In dominantly Christian countries only skeptics and heretics thought otherwise.

Among scientists of the Victorian era there was caused by evolutionism a further confounding of confusion of the subject of life. The undeviating materialists saw Darwin's research as the vindication of their position: namely, that organic life in its molecular simplicity arose spontaneously by chemical action; that it developed and diversified over aeons of aeons into myriad species with mutants still forming; that only by chance and through fortuitous change did evolution take place; and that eventually scientific investigation will explain even so fugitive a problem as the development of consciousness in human beings. Yet some materialists deviated from this new orthodoxy to the extent that they acknowledged a purpose in organic evolution. Darwin himself was perplexed. First, he wrote in 1870, "I cannot look at the universe as the result of blind chance," but then he conceded, "yet I see no evidence of beneficent design, or indeed of design of any kind, in the details."[24] Nevertheless, two of Darwin's strongest, famous supporters, the British biologist Thomas Henry Huxley and the American botanist Asa Gray, rejoiced in "Darwin's great service to Natural Science in bringing back to it Teleology," as the latter wrote in 1874.[25]

What they meant by this estimate of evolutionary thought depends, of course, upon the content of the word teleology. They did not mean it in terms of the biblical faith in God's ultimate, or eschatological, purpose for individuals, the elect, or all humanity. Nor, we may assume, did they have the entelechy of Aristotle in mind—the power of fulfillment of an organism. In fact, a mixture of these two concepts did gain much popularity because of Darwinism, a doctrine persisting for decades as "Social Darwinism." This was the application of the idea of teleological evolution to society and culture. The view was epitomized by the benign philosophy of Herbert Spencer and widely accepted as an optimistic faith in inevitable progress toward a kind of kingdom of God on earth. (Was it merely coincidence that it thrived during the euphoric decades of the British Empire's power and America's expansion?) But the teleology to which Huxley and Gray alluded was defined by a goal which seems more suited to the anxious minds of many people today—that is, species survival. What Huxley called "the telic aspect of organic phenomena" means just this and no more. "Since mutation and selection are held to be *the* major mechanisms of evolution," writes Marjorie Grene of this view, "and evolution the mechanism by which life has come to exist and survives, whatever exists in the organic world has been and is a *means* to survival as its *end*."[26]

The struggle for survival has surely been demonstrated in the case of numerous species, including Homo sapiens; and so has the chemistry of matter been shown to be indispensable to all life. Is that enough to say about life in general from a scientific standpoint? Some now think it is. But the twentieth century began without a consensus among the experts, even though a vast amount of new biological knowledge had been harvested in the century since Kant's death in 1804. And a consensus still eludes us.

Looking back on the nearly hundred years since Darwin's publication, the eminent evolutionary anthropologist George Gaylord Simpson summed up his understanding of human life with magisterial authority as follows:

> Man is the result of a purposeless and materialistic process that did not have him in mind. He was not planned. He is a state of matter, a form of life, a sort of animal, and a species of the Order Primates, akin nearly or remotely to all of life and indeed to all that is material. It is, however, a gross misrepresentation to say that he is *just* an accident or *nothing* but an animal . . . man is unique . . . the highest form of organization of matter and energy that has ever appeared.[27]

This statement would once have been just as shocking to human, humane, and humanistic sensibilities as de la Mettrie's human machine was. Today it is representative of widely accepted thought. If biologists are asked to define "life" today, they would probably reply, writes C. U. M. Smith, "by describing the nature of self-replicating molecules, of energy-rich phosphate bonds and the mechanism of Darwinian evolution."[28]

Is this not sheer materialism? Yes, it is. Must not, therefore, a philosopher who accepts metaphysics, religious or not, reject such materialism? Not necessarily. At least, there are respected philosophers and theologians who espouse such a view. Professor A. R. Peacocke of England, who is both a biochemist and a theologian, declares that we may "regard living organisms *as matter organized in a special manner* and not as matter invested with a special property 'life' beyond the scope of the physical sciences."[29] He is thus ready and disposed to discard the prevalent theological view, which was shared equally by Christians of learned sophistication and conventional belief until quite recently. They would have sided readily with the statement made in 1890 by another natural scientist and influential theologian Henry Drummond:

> This inorganic world is staked off from the living world by barriers which have never yet been crossed from within. No change of substance, no modification of environment, no chemistry, no electricity, nor any form of energy, nor any evolution can endow any single atom of the mineral world with the attribute of Life. Only by the bending down into this dead world of some living form can these

dead atoms be gifted with the properties of vitality; without this preliminary contact with Life they remain fixed in the inorganic sphere forever.[30]

At the time Drummond wrote these self-assured words there was a prominent scientist in Germany who was coming to embrace the vitalist theory with tenacity and passion equal to Drummond's. This was Hans Driesch of Heidelberg, a zoologist who became professor of philosophy. He claimed to have come to the vitalist theory, not by speculation, but by critical deduction from evidences resulting from his experiments in the embryology and replicating morphology of hydroid polyps, echinoderms such as sea urchins, as well as frogs. What impressed him was the invariable way in which each specimen, however damaged or truncated, kept striving to grow toward a whole organism. For Driesch this compulsion to grow into the proper shape of the species could be attributed only to "the *autonomy of life*, i.e. the doctrine of so-called vitalism"; for he concluded, "there is some agent at work in morphogenesis which is not of the type of physico-chemical agents."[31]

Driesch's rejection of merely mechanical material causation for morphogenesis was reinforced by his study of human behavior, especially neural responses which involved consciousness. His reflections on human nature pointed in the same direction: *Something* else is at work. Of this he was sure. But Driesch summoned neither a transcendental psychic power nor a divine spirit or will to provide an answer to the nagging question of what or who supplied vitality. In an attitude of respectful agnosticism toward such an ultimate question he was content to rehabilitate the name, if not the concept, of Aristotle's entelechy, without presuming to define it.[32] "We are therefore *absolutely unable to say anything whatever* about the origin of life," he conceded. "Life is there," however, "and is transferred from generation to generation in material continuity."[33] But there is nothing to be found in Darwinian literature to suggest an explanation of origins.

On first reading Driesch, one thinks that he was merely reasserting the truth of vitalism in contrast to the inevitability of a wholly mechanistic materialistic view, which is condemned as false. On further reading, however, this categorical distinction is seen not to be present. In the view of the critical savant of biology Hellmuth Plessner, Driesch did not mean that life without entelechy is reduced to self-motivated matter.[34] The universal consciousness of what it means for a person to be alive rules out such a crass reductionism. But Driesch's preference for an unknowable superadded vital force to make matter come alive and keep alive seemed merely to beg the question. Perhaps in his agnosticism as a biologist-philosopher he was groping for the knowledge of microbiology, virology, and genetics which became available fifty years later. Meanwhile he contended against mechanism and materialism with the vigor of a prophet—but one who could not truly say, "Thus saith the Lord." And he advocated vitalism with the zeal of an apostle, yet commending it only as "a sort of label affixed to our ignorance," as Henri Bergson called it, the purpose of which is to remind us of this ignorance lest we "ignore that ignorance" as mechanism invites us to do.[35]

Bergson, the leading French philosopher of the early twentieth century, enjoyed a popularity that cannot be exaggerated. The depth of his influence on Western European, British, and American intellectuals could be compared to that of his younger countryman, Pierre Teilhard de Chardin, a generation later. Both of these daring thinkers taught human evolution in a novel way, giving people an optimistic, hopeful view of the history and destiny of humanity. This came at a time when the optimism engendered by Social Darwinism was being tempered, in part, and rendered ambiguous by the scientists' reduction of claims for intrinsic human superiority. The naturalistic idea of human life as deriving from physicochemical sources, and only from these, was a severe threat to the sense of human identity. It remains so today.

The nub of Bergson's thought about the famous *élan vital* cannot be found so concisely expressed in his own *Creative Evolution* as it is when encapsulated by one of his most mordant contemporary critics, Bertrand Russell:

> The whole universe is the clash and conflict of two opposite motions: life, which climbs upwards, and matter, which falls downward. Life is one great force, one vast vital impulse, given once and for all from the beginning of the world, meeting the resistance of matter, strug-

gling to break a way through matter, learning gradually to use matter by means of organization. . . . retaining always its capacity for free activity, struggling always to find new outlets, seeking always for greater liberty of movement amid the opposing walls of matter.[36]

Unimpressed by this concept of the primordial life force, Russell dismissed it with a devastating epithet: "an anti-intellectual philosophy."[37] Moreover, his rejection is not compelled by a materialistic bias, but rather by a concern to defend human dignity. We would, he charged, "be the blind slaves of instinct: the lifeforce pushes us on from behind, restlessly and unceasingly. There is no room in this philosophy for the moment of contemplative insight when, in rising above the animal life, we become conscious of the greater ends that redeem man from the life of the brutes."[38]

The infectious power of vitalism as an explanatory theory of life was felt at the opening of the twentieth century in literature as well as in science and philosophy. The brilliant dramatist and social satirist George Bernard Shaw found vitalism to be not only the explanation of the sexual drive for survival of the species but also the clue to human behavior in respect to personal relations, social dynamics, politics, and philosophical reflection.

In one of the most sparkling, extended dialogues in dramatic literature, Act III of *Man and Superman*, Shaw has cast into hell the cast of Mozart's *Don Giovanni* and added the devil as their host and partner in conversation. In the eternal placidity and boredom of this Shavian sheol, Don Juan becomes Shaw's philosopher of the life force, while the devil represents Darwinian mechanism. He acknowledges that the amorous compulsion that drove him to one thousand and three conquests in Spain—to say nothing of other international affairs—was not his romantic yearning for the ideal woman's love, or the ideal love of a woman. It was just "the universal creative energy" which can throw utter strangers into an embrace "at the exchange of a glance." "Life cannot will its own extinction," says Don Juan to a skeptical devil, who argues that "the power that governs the earth is not the power of Life but of Death." No, Life is "the force that ever strives to attain greater power of contemplating itself." Self-consciousness is thus placed at the summit of the evolutionary sequence of cellular, organic, vertebrate, and cerebral life. "Life is a force which has made innumerable experiments in organizing itself: . . . the mammoth and the man, the mouse and the megatherium, the flies and the fleas and the Fathers of the Church are all more or less successful attempts to build up that raw force into higher and higher individuals."[39] When pious Donna Anna protests his including the Fathers of the Church with the flies and the fleas, Don Juan explains that it was only for the purposes of alliteration!

The ironic humor of Shaw earned him a lasting reputation as the consummate debunker of the conventional prejudices and half-baked ideas that constitute the mentality and speech of the masses. So it is the more ironical that he embraced what may be called the "bio-sophical" doctrine of the life force just when it was being debunked by biological scientists generally. What if Shaw had also professed the Christian belief in the once-for-all creation of all living things and with it the overflowing of God's animating power for sustaining all living organisms? Then he would have found himself in the strange company of doctrinal defenders who, more than a century after Darwin, are still embattled against biological mechanism and purposeless evolution. However, there was no danger of that for the Irish wit. He agreed with Driesch and Bergson that a vigorous vitalism requires no divine source or sustenance. This secular appeal to an undefined and undefinable life force nevertheless could not spare these and all vitalists the ridicule and scorn of many biologists who prevailed at the end of the nineteenth century.

That century, observed William Coleman, presented "a bewildering variety of vitalisms and mechanisms."[40] On both sides stood biologists who were professionally at home in the field or laboratory rather than in academic chairs of philosophy or theology. So both sides believed that their concepts of life were derived from empirical observation, description, and analysis rather than from intuition or revelation. The steep and commanding ascendancy of scientific materialism during the twentieth century has obviously been such as to inform the thinking of the greater number of scientists. Any theories of vitalism, therefore, be they supernatural, metaphysical, or rooted somehow in molecular structure, have been branded either heretical, obsolescent, or extinct. Among biologists today the very word "vitalism" has become either a joke or a kind of obscenity.

In the opinion of perhaps most of the experts, the merely theoretical rejection of vitalism until 1953 gave way thereafter to its practical destruction. The outstanding British biochemist Francis Crick, who shared the glory of discovering the secret of the molecule of deoxyribonucleic acid (DNA), believes that he thus took part in the complete and final defeat of vitalistic thinking. Since his and James Watson's achievement in 1953 microbiology has provided, in the words of Gunther S. Stent, "the molecular genetic interment of vitalism."[41] The idea of a mysterious vital force, "which Crick identifies with Christianity, and especially with Catholicism," concludes Stent, "has now, at last, been definitely smashed."[42] Likewise, the French biochemist Jacques Monod, in his widely debated essay *Chance and Necessity*, has apparently punctured the bright balloons of his countrymen— Bergson's evolutionary vitalism, and the cosmic "animism" (as Monod calls it) of Teilhard de Chardin's vision.[43] Neither of these could withstand the pricking of the sharp instrument of scientific knowledge, which modern microbiologists accept as dogma: "that all the properties of living beings rest on *a fundamental mechanism of molecular invariance.*"[44]

The rapidly unfolding knowledge of the chemical structure and function of genes and chromosomes is clearly having an impact upon our thinking about life, an impact that should be at least equivalent to that of Darwinism. Public concern about the biophilosophical implications of the genetic revolutions, however, is much less agitated and clamorous than was that about evolution. The explanation for this relatively small concern lies partly in the far broader extent of scientific education, which today is more widespread than that of the nineteenth century. A less obvious yet major factor must be the vast difference in visibility and conceptualizability. People can look at an ape or a chimpanzee and become highly disturbed and affronted at the suggestion that we are but a lofty branch on the tree of mammalian primates. When we are told, however, that the chemical elements of the trillions of genes in our body cells are the same as in the genes of all living organisms, and that the subatomic electric charges determine the function of our genes just as they do for dandelions, centipedes, and rats, how can our minds grasp and reflect upon such data? The measurements are too small, the quantities too large, the implications too unsettling.

Even if our minds can be educated to comprehend such information, as though seeing the invisible, must we concede that these physicochemical phenomena are all that constitute life? The twenty amino acids which together make a molecule of protein can theoretically be compacted under the right conditions of heat, pressure, and environment to produce protein, that unit of living matter. If this should be successfully achieved in a laboratory, will the idea of materialistic mechanism have been proved categorically to be true?

THE ROLE OF FAITH

In the last analysis—at least, in the present stage of humanity's knowledge—it is only by an act of faith that we can postulate the source, power, and purpose of organic life and especially of the highly developed species culminating in humanity. This is an accepted idea for persons who are of metaphysical, idealist, or religious persuasions. For them it is intellectually repugnant to assert that every living tissue and sentient response and conscious action can be reduced to materialistic and mechanistic causes. Whatever have been the vulnerable weaknesses of several vitalistic theories and beliefs, they have been put forth in the modern era as reaction against the unsatisfying claims of materialists as well as their candid avoidance of persistent questions about life. John B. Habgood, a biologist and theologian, rightly observes that "most of us feel very deeply that physics and chemistry are not enough to explain life. Vitalism tries to express this feeling scientifically. . . it is a negative protest, an expostulation that physicists and chemists ought not to be allowed to have it their own way."[45]

Is the materialist's claim also an exercise in faith, despite all disclaimers? So it appears. The widely acclaimed, comprehensive scientist Carl Sagan scorns all vitalistic, metaphysical, or religious pretensions. "Indeed, there is nothing debasing in the thought that man is made of atoms alone," he writes. No, that is not a debasing thought if the human body as physical organism is meant. There are an estimated seven octillion (7×10^{27}) atoms in a human adult, making ten trillion (10^{13}) cells, and that is cause for utmost amazement at our physical nature.[46] But Sagan is clearly thinking of the totality of a human life when he expresses something like a doxology and confesses faith: "What a wonder that atoms can be put together in so complex a pattern as to produce man. Man is a tribute to the subtlety of matter."[47]

So the agelong argument which began in Greece with Democritus will not have been won when his present followers are able to marshal all the scientifically accepted facts about molecular biology and its ramifications. The ontological distance between a molecule of protein and the man Plato is just too great. At the molecular level there can be no question anymore that the mechanisms provide what may be called the basic pulses of organic life of every kind. But the formidable distance between human genes and human geniuses, or even ordinary people, has not been tracked. Neither microbiology nor the whole body of scientific literature on evolution and development can account for a person's writing this sentence—or for a million other functions.

3

RECOVERING
THE HEBRAIC INSIGHT:
LIFE IS UNITARY

THE INTERACTION OF BIOLOGICAL AND
THEOLOGICAL KNOWLEDGE

Is human life a "tribute to the subtlety of matter?" Or is matter a tribute to the cosmic intelligence and creativity of God?

The polarities presented in the previous chapter may seem to defy any resolution of the opposition between the general categories of mechanism and vitalism. They constitute a standoff between the life sciences and theistic religion, if indeed mechanism is assumed to be the theory that is most appropriate to science, and if some kind of vitalism—by whatever name—is intrinsic to religious interpretation of reality. On the surface at least the perennial debate seems to regard the mechanism-vitalism dichotomy as unbridgeable—two mutually exclusive beliefs about organic life. Seen this way, there are only two alternatives. One is to make categorical claims for the truth either of materialism as the basis and essence of life, or of biblical revelation as the adequate explanation of life and species; this plainly means that a person adhering to one position rejects the other completely. The other option, however, is to decide that the scientific dimension and the religious dimension of knowledge refer to two entirely different realities—one to the natural order of matter, the other to the realm of spiritual life.

In neither of these two ways of regarding life is there the possibility of perceiving an interaction between empirical evidence of phenomena and belief in divine creativity. Yet, there must be a recognition of such interaction if we are to be intellectually serious about both the massive and marvelous data accumulated by scientific research and our own observations and reflections on those manifestations of life and behavior which point beyond materialism for explanation.[1]

In accepting the interaction of biological and theological knowledge we need not betray the consistency of our own reasoning, obscure and difficult as some problems may be; neither must we take refuge in a dualistic notion that avoids at the outset any possible difficulty. We can affirm at one and the same time the validity of scientific observations on the physicochemical nature of molecules, cells, and organisms, including humans, as well as the wisdom of received biblical religion concerning the character of all life and especially the human.

Religious thinkers and theologians have much to be modest about when they compare the results of their often haphazard, uncritical study and reflection with the prodigious investigations made by psychologists, geneticists, microbiologists, neurologists, and anthropologists. In past centuries, theologians were notorious for their arrogant condescension toward the natural and social sciences. In retrospect, we judge that there was never any justification for that conceit of omniscience. Vestiges of such imperialism remain today, not on the part of judicious theologians but on the part of uncritical biblicists and dogmatists. However, it is generally the case that the table of history has turned against the advocates of religiously conditioned knowledge in favor of the secular philosophers and scientists. Today it is enough to satisfy well-informed religious thinkers if they can enjoy a fair hearing and a dialogue with others on equal footing.

Michael Landmann, a philosophical anthropologist, is objectively correct when he writes: "The oldest information about man is contained in the religions."[2] More debatable is the question of whether this ancient information still has contemporary pertinence and value. Is it at all fruitful to explore the old traditions of Judaism and Christianity, which more than any others have shaped the religious insights about life in Western civilization? Or is it a waste of time to seek usable concepts for today in the Bible and in the voluminous teaching of scholars of these faiths? A positive or negative answer to these questions depends, of course, upon the personal religious beliefs or sympathies of those who address them. To weigh the religious teachings about human life without any bias or presupposition is manifestly impossible. They have to be presented quite literally "for what they are worth." This may be very little for some and much indeed for others. The critical divide is the affirmation or disavowal of a transcendent power—God—which, or who, has anything to do with the creation, nature and destiny of human beings. Yet, even those who are reluctant to declare their belief in the personal divine Creator, as well as those who firmly reject such belief, are often influenced deeply in their thinking about human life by the old religious teachings. This is especially true of some idealistic humanists in Euro-American cultures, which have been informed to a large extent, first, by Jewish and then by Christian faith. The discussion here will be limited to these two inseparable biblical religions.

CHRISTIAN CONFUSION OF THE
BIBLICAL UNITY

How do fundamental insights come to a people? By the accumulation of corporate experience and wisdom? By the brilliant teaching of a few outstanding philosophers? People of faith say that their insights come by revelation from God. The distinctive understanding of human life presented in the Bible—explicitly in some places and implicitly throughout—which includes the doctrine of the creation of man, is a Hebraic insight interpreted by faith as a matter of revelation. A historical and critical reading of the Bible does not exclude revelation, but takes account as well of the cultural context and communal experience within which the biblical texts evolved.

The preeminent feature of early Israel's becoming a particular people within a Mediterranean area where polytheism was rife was its assertion of monotheism and its intensifying emphasis upon the divine uniqueness and unity: "Hear, O Israel: The Lord our God is one Lord" ran the much-repeated *Shema* (Deut. 6:4). This rigorous monotheism pervaded Hebrew belief, thought, and culture. It allowed no place for pluralism or even dualism in the conceptions of either God or man. In the words of a prominent British rabbi who writes on medical ethics, both the unity of the human being and the unity of religion, morality, and hygiene "are the direct consequence of the doctrine of absolute monotheism."[3] One God meant one life. The characteristics of this unitary anthropology will be considered shortly.

Let it be noted, meanwhile, that many Gentile Christians today assume that they know what the Hebraic, biblical understanding of human life is, when in fact they innocently deceive themselves. These are persons who postulate the dualism that splits spirit and matter, separates soul and body, sunders the immortal life from the mortal. Whenever religion is thought to have concern with "spiritual realities" only, whatever is material is logically excluded from the religious perspective on human life and experience. Such is a most common but erroneous idea of what Judaism and Christianity mean. It is held by many Christians, who have thus given to observers outside the church the notion that Christianity is in fact dualistic. Actually, this dualism stems from an ancient and pervasive strain of Greek philosophy, not from a biblical theology or anthropology.

It is easy, and not entirely inaccurate, to lay this deception to Plato and to the perennial attractiveness of Platonism. Plato indeed stands in the history of philosophy and religion as the epitome of those numerous thinkers—Greek, Hindu, Gentile Christian, and even Jewish—who have held that the immortal "soul" is the absolutely good form, essence, idea, or reality, while the material body is crude, wasting, corruptible, finite, and essentially evil.

Shrouded in the uncertain haze of mythology, the religion of Orpheus gave prominence to the Greek dualism. As a philosopher and authority on Gnosticism, Hans Jonas observes:

> Sōma—sema, the body—a tomb: this Orphic formula expressed the first dualistic answer to the problem of death. . . . the body as such is the grave of the soul, and bodily death is the latter's resurrection. Life dwells like a stranger in the flesh which by its own nature— the nature of the corporeal—is nothing but corpse, seemingly alive by favor of the soul's passing presence in it. Only in death, relinquished by its alien visitor, does the body return to its original truth, and soul to hers.[4]

This belief in the utter discontinuity between spiritual soul and physical body was not so categorical in Plato's own thought, or in that of Athens' golden age as is now popularly assumed; however, it was strong enough to give rise to thoroughgoing dualisms in subsequent eras.

A ready clue to this Hellenic insight is found in the marvelous sculpture of ancient Greece. The Greeks were obviously devoted admirers of the beauty of the human body. Their athletes disciplined body muscles and controlled body fats. Their fashion designers clothed the body with flattering drapery, freely exhibiting its most pleasing curvatures. And their peerless sculptors turned Pentelic marble and cast bronze into idealized paragons of corporal perfection. The handsome gods and goddesses of Mount Olympus inspired emulation by mortals who trained for the Olympic Games. Adonis, Aphrodite, Apollo, and Artemis remain today in our vocabulary as synonyms for physical excellence. Exceptions were made, as in the case of drunken Bacchus, when human debasement rather than divine perfection was intended.

Nevertheless, the Greeks always exalted the superiority of the soul over the body. What they called the soul's *erōs*, its upward striving for divine perfection, presupposed its final emancipation from the body through death. The aesthetic appeal of beautiful faces and forms, inseparable from sexual attraction, was subordinate to the belief that the body was merely an earthly vessel of the eternal soul. There was a double imaging, though: the soul was the image of the gods; the body was the transient and mortal image of the soul. However lowly and corruptible flesh and bone may be, though, they were held by Plato "to be nurtured with care and clothed with honor."[5]

Plato's dualism did not imply a deliberate denial of health or abhorrence of natural tendencies to appreciate and admire the body. Though Plato did not despise the body, he still considered the immortal reality of the self to reside in the soul. Otherwise, the self would perish when the body dies, as the materialists have always taught.

While the Hebraic conception of the unity of the human person was becoming integrated and fixed in the biblical texts, Greek thought was moving in two divergent directions. In one way, thanks largely to Aristotle's empirical observations of animals and humans and reflections upon the substantial soul, or animating force, in all living things, positive affirmation was given to the body of flesh and bone and to the matter of how it is composed. In his view, "the soul cannot be without a body, while it cannot be a body; it is not a body but something relative to a body."[6] Distinct but inseparable are soul and body; but there is no reason to demean or denigrate the value of the body.

The other movement of Hellenic thought extended the Platonic dualism to an extreme conclusion, to hylophobia, or the fear and utter distaste for matter. Less than five centuries after Plato this pessimism about the body had reached the point where "matter is inherently evil and the source of moral evil," a view which, according to A. E. Taylor, was "wholly incompatible with the genuine doctrine of Plato."[7] Genuine or not, it was this morbid distortion of Plato's dualism that reached its maximum power in the religious movements known as Gnosticism. Gnosticism infected some forms of Jewish thought as well as the rising belief and theology of Christianity. In the city of Alexandria on the Nile delta, this radical dualism of soul and body was already having its deepest impact on Jewish thought during the lifetime of Jesus of Nazareth. The influential philosopher, Philo, was persuaded, in effect, that Moses and Plato could be perfectly harmonized. But this harmonization was achieved by surrendering the Hebraic to the Hellenic world view and anthropology. For Philo, a Greek-speaking and Greek-thinking Jew, the only true life (*zōē*) is eternal, free of time and space, while the mortal life (*bios*) is a deplorable state of captivity from which the soul (*psuchē*) strives to escape. The emancipation can come only through the successful effort in time, through discipline and asceticism, to achieve purity; and, failing this in one lifetime, the soul must transmigrate to another in order to continue the *erōs* striving.[8]

After the second century, in the same Egyptian city, this Greek dualism was assimilated and effectively taught by Clement, Origen, Cyril, and the heretical Arius. Latin theology after the fourth century in Italy and North Africa was similarly shaped by Augustine. Thus began and flourished the long tradition of Christian asceticism, monasticism, mysticism, celibacy, otherworldliness, and longing for escape from earth to heaven and eternal bliss. Christians initiated by baptism forswore "the world, the flesh, and the devil," an unholy trinity of corruption which dragged like heavy chains upon the soul in need of salvation. In fact, Christianity as a whole has never succeeded in resolving the manifest tensions between soul and body, spirit and matter. Neoplatonism remains in conflict today with the Hebraic insight into God's good creation and the unity of the human person.

This struggle was vividly reflected in the two centuries of dispute over the reality of the person of Jesus Christ as both human and divine. Its canonical settlement by the Council of Chalcedon in A.D. 451 was achieved by the use of paradox: Jesus as the Christ was confessed as being one person having both divine and human natures. Those who taught that he was only a divine person were considered to be just as heretical as those who believed him to have been human only. This christological debate, protracted and perplexing as it was, and still incomprehensible to many, was unavoidable in view of the apostolic and New Testament witnesses to Jesus.

By analogy, it can be seen how the continuing dispute over the relation of soul and body in the human person raised similar questions. Whenever in the history of the church there arose a dominant tendency to deny the body and all matter in favor of the soul or what is "spiritual," the strain upon the tension between them became too great. Then the church's remembered Hebraic anthropology returned in strength and caused these tendencies to be called heretical. Gnostics of the second century, Arians of the fourth, and the Cathari or Albigenses of the thirteenth century were rejected, persecuted and excommunicated because, apart from other cultural and political reasons, their teachings contradicted the biblically proclaimed goodness of God's creation and of mortal man as God's creature. Eastern Orthodoxy was also split in controversy over the Hesychast movement, a mystical reassertion of the Neoplatonic dualism. Churches of the sixteenth-century Reformation were obliged to contend with the same kinds of dispute. Martin Luther stoutly resisted the swarms of pesky "enthusiasts" (*Schwärmer*) and "spiritualists," whose piety not only negated the material and zesty life which for Luther was a

63

gift from God but also threatened the historical reality of Jesus Christ and the church as well. Luther's rival in reforming, John Calvin, however, was still committed to the dualism of Plato, who might have written these very words in Calvin's great treatise on doctrine:

> When the soul is freed from the prison-house of the body, God becomes its perpetual keeper . . . [and] occupies the body as a kind of habitation.[9]

This helps explain why Calvin also interpreted the nature of the church in a dualistic way, drawing a distinction between the "visible church" and the "invisible church." In modern times, this generic Hellenism with its asymmetrical dualism has reappeared within Christianity among the Quakers, Shakers, and Christian Scientists, to the consternation of strict adherents of biblical religion.

The infusion of this ultraplatonic doctrine of the soul into Christian thinking, along with its intensifying denigration of the physical body, thus compromised and distorted the Hebraic insight at an early date. It is no wonder that the third-century Latin theologian Tertullian posed the question which has been asked repeatedly since: What has Athens to do with Jerusalem? Nor is it strange that numerous present-day Christians cannot distinguish the Hellenic and Hebraic elements of their theology, doctrine, or personal religious thought. Indeed, writing a century later Cyril of Jerusalem admonished the candidates for baptism:

> Know that thou art a two-fold man consisting of soul and body, and that the same God is the Artificer both of the soul and the body. . . . Endure not any of those who say that the body belongs not to God; for they who hold this, and that the soul dwells in it as in a vessel which belongeth not to itself, readily abuse it to fornication.[10]

The numerous present-day Christians and others who tacitly think of the body-soul dualism as defining human life may not, as a consequence, resort to fornication, but they inevitably have difficulty in grasping the meaning of life in the Hebrew Scriptures and the New Testament.

When for example the account of the creation of Adam in the Book of Genesis is read today, it seems quite natural to understand the story in a dualistic, Hellenic manner. Where the text says, "the Lord God formed man of dust from the ground," is not this dust obviously corruptible matter? And when God "breathed into his nostrils the breath of life," is not this breath the eternal, immortal soul (Gen. 2:7)? Or when "breath" leaves the body at the time of death, literally at the body's expiration, is it not congruent with the Old Testament insight to say that the immortal soul is escaping from its temporary, mortal prison house? Death scenes in medieval and Renaissance paintings often showed the soul as a vapor rising from the mouth or nostrils of the corpse. In the same Platonic style, icons depicting the "falling asleep" of the virgin Mary portrayed Jesus by the bedside, holding in his arms the baby that was her immortal soul. Such naive, simplistic dualism is conceivable and appealing; but it is not the biblical mode of understanding human life.

LIFE AS CONCRETE EXISTENCE

A hundred generations before the rise of modern psychiatry, the Hebraic mind recognized that human life is psychosomatic. When a contemporary philosopher can assert bluntly, *"Psuchē and sōma* are inextricably bound together as constituents of an integral context in all living humans,"[11] he is declaring a biblical concept having important implications for modern science as well as for religious belief. Those who read the archetypal myth of the creation of Adam as a dualistic theory of the animation of the inanimate body may appear on the surface to be legitimately justified. The *anima*, or *psuchē*, is then regarded as the only proper human entity to be valued, while the body is expendable. Or else, if the analogy of the breath of life is exchanged for the nearly universal metaphor of fire, one can see the creation of Adam as the implanting of a divine spark from the sunlike divinity, which is the source, reason, and goal of all life. But this old notion of Heraclitus and the Stoic philosophers is as foreign to the biblical concept as is the Platonic. Both of these presume to postulate a vital energy which is external to the physiological body. Dualistic views have differed concerning the relation of the soul, or breath of life or fire, to the material organism. Some emphasize the incongruity and estrangement; others the compatibility and harn.ony. In either instance, however, there is no recognition of the essential unity of the human person. Human life according to biblical thinking is monistic, unitary. It is the concrete existence of the whole human being. Rather than connoting an invisible, timeless soul which temporarily inhabits a mortal organism, life means temporality, spatiality, mobility, self-direction. Human life is movement in time and space of the being who is both flesh and spirit, both body and soul, at once and intrinsically.[12]

This ancient insight may indeed coincide with some modern views that hold life to be holistic and unitary, or psychosomatic. The Jews did not grasp and refine this insight by reflecting upon data of biology and psychology, scientifically gathered and interpreted. It was a concomitant of Israel's faith in Yahweh. He was known as the *living* God, the Creator who is thus the *life-giving* God, the *life-preserving* God. It is common enough for Jewish and Christian people, or those influenced by such faiths, to say that "life is a gift of God." This appears to be a truism for those who hold such faith, but the statement requires closer scrutiny. In biblical understanding it is not quite accurate to say that in the creation of Adam and Eve, or of any person, Yahweh merely imparts or bestows the initial energizing quality called life, embracing both the biological and the psychic. According to a carefully discriminated nuance, by contrast, God in the Bible *makes alive.* Adam did not *receive* a living soul, or *nēpēs*; he *became* a living soul. By exerting the same creative power, clothed in personal love for the creature, God sustains the life that he has made. For this reason, the value of life is never independent or intrinsically cherishable by itself, for it always remains relative to the providential care and purposeful will of Yahweh. The vitality of human life, then, can never be isolated from the meaning of its existence, whether potentially or actually experienced.

A defection from this understanding is illustrated by the most famous of all paintings of the creation—the majestic fresco in the Sistine Chapel of the Vatican palace. Michelangelo's painting shows Yahweh in the act of creating Adam. The anthropomorphic depicting of God as the Cosmic Grandfather is hardly acceptable to reasonable minds today; but that question need not deter us here. Neither must Adam's navel be regarded as evidence that the great artist was intending to dispute or ridicule the myth of Adam's having had no mother. Our attention focuses, rather, upon the two index fingers, the Creator's and the creature's. Adam's is limp; God's is assertive. The fingers are close but do not touch. It seems as if a high-voltage arc light is about to flash between their tips as the vital energy of life is transmitted. Commenting upon an interpretation of this familiar picture as written by F. J. J. Buytendijk, Marjorie Grene explains that this "represents so superbly the achievements of humanity through the body's taking on of a spiritual life."[13] If her words repeat the thought of the artist, as well they might, they only indicate what Michelangelo's other heroic persons on the ceiling (including the judging Christ) also show—that his muscular figures would have been more at home on Mount Olympus than on Mount Zion. The Sistine Adam is not a whole, integrated human being, but a material body waiting to be animated. Michelangelo's Bible is Hellenic, not Hebraic.

The Jewishness of the contemporary painter Marc Chagall is never more evident than in the stark contrast between his modern picture of the creation of Adam and that of the Renaissance giant. Chagall's drawing is for a series of biblical illustrations. In the center, held tenderly in the arms of an angel of Yahweh, the complete man Adam is being made alive. But two symbolic images in the background catch our eyes. They are unexpected and, at first thought, out of place. One image is the double stone tablet of the Law, the Decalogue, which is held by two hands extended down from heaven. The other, suspended in air, is the crucified Jesus (the figure with which Chagall seems to be obsessed). What could these pivotal symbols representing respectively the Old Testament and the New have to do with the origin of man and the beginning of human life? Why the Torah and the cross? One can offer a conjecture, knowing well enough that viewers who interpret pictures often claim to find more or different meaning than the artist intended.

The human race, which Adam represents as its mythical progenitor, is not called into being merely for the purpose of existing and surviving in the manner of all other animal life. God means that human life is to be life with a distinct purpose, with direction and goal. So Chagall locates the Garden of Eden in relation to two other places of high ground which are decisive for all history—Mount Sinai and a hill outside Jerusalem called Calvary. Adam's race is being made alive in order to accept the binding covenant with Yahweh which is mediated by Moses, and then to learn the way to the fulfillment of love through suffering, as epitomized by the death of Jesus. Lest this seem to imply a Jew's concession to Christianity's claims for Jesus' death, Hans Küng points out that Marc Chagall "constantly represented the sufferings of his people in the image of the Crucified."[14]

The biblical concept of life, then, cannot be separated from the concern that in modern jargon has come to be known as "quality of life." The infusion of vital energy or the breath of life into a man-shaped lump of clay suggests a dualism which is not intended in Genesis and which fails to convey the meaning of human life that is basic to the entire biblical story and faith. So, quality of life is not measured by the degree of satisfaction of elemental needs and desires, such as all animals have, or by a hedonistic feeling of pleasure. It is defined and measured instead by the living out day by day of the Creator's expectations, which are intensely moral. Life is not only holistic in the sense of being the integration of the whole person; it is also holy because its deepest meaning consists of being in accord with the Creator's purpose. It is on this premise that people who accept the Hebraic view with all its implications are able to speak quite literally of the "sanctity of life."

HEBREW WORDS FOR
UNIVERSAL MEANINGS

The Hebrew Bible presents no systematic treatise, no sustained discourse, no argumentation on its anthropology. This is not the biblical mode of conveying ideas. In the history and metahistory that its many books narrate, however, along with all the characterizations of persons and the varied expressions of authentic human experience, it presents the Hebraic concept of human life.

Various words are used to speak of life, but not one has the sharpened definition that philosophers and scientists would demand. Some of these Hebrew words are sufficiently similar to the Greek so that it has been too easy, and almost unavoidable, for Hellenic and Platonic constructions to be placed upon them. When *nēpēs* is rendered simply as "soul" or *ruah* as "spirit" it is natural to assume that these are the equivalents of the Greek *psuchē* and *pneuma*. Then one might expect to find some Hebrew word like the Greek *sōma* for "body" which the soul or spirit, in Greek fashion, could animate. It is both strange and highly significant, however, that biblical Hebrew has no common or exact word for the body. This leaves the Hellenized mind wondering how the Hebraic mind understood human life. That wonder is allayed only when one enters into the Hebrew way, which is also the original Christian way, of conceiving life. The Bible speaks often of "flesh" (*basar*) as "the individual being in its earthly condition,"[15] or *basar* is conjoined with "bone" as descriptive of a person's body, or *basar* may refer to all humanity as "flesh." Otherwise, by the use of synecdoche a number of parts of the organism—such as the belly, the back, the thigh, or the bones— can express the whole body. Therefore, the boundary between flesh and body always remains indistinct. A body in contrast to a soul is foreign to this Hebraic mentality.[16]

Nēpēs

The Hebrew word commonly understood as "life" is *nēpēs*, which the older English translators rendered in hundreds of instances as "soul." Soul can be one of its meanings, of course, but a plasticity of meaning is equally permissible. *Nēpēs*, for example, refers also to the whole form of man, including such physical parts as the throat and neck as well as the attached organs of breathing and feeding, which are indispensable for life. Also, it means the whole range of feelings and desires which express the sensibilities of the living person. So *nēpēs* gathers a number of attributes and parts which add up to the wholeness of human life itself; and this means not only the individual person but also the collective or corporate life of the people. In brief, an individual human being is not a *nēpēs* having a body, nor a body joined to

69

a *nēpeš*. According to the clear analysis of Hans-Walter Wolff, *nēpeš* is not a kind of "indestructible core of being, in contradistinction to physical life."[17] Human beings do not just have *nēpeš*; they are *nēpeš*. If the word were adequately rendered "soul," we have colloquial expressions which seem to say the same: "There are two thousand souls in this village," but in saying that, we do not mean to exclude their bodies—we mean two thousand lives.

Ruah

Equally frequent in the Scriptures is the word *ruah*, usually translated "spirit" or "breath." Its root meaning is like that of the Greek *pneuma*—the wind or the breath. *Ruah* is often used literally for these related phenomena. But the word also conveys the sense of spontaneity of life, especially when it is conjoined with the word "life," which is *hayyim*. So the "breath of life" is—for both humans and animals—the very continuity of being alive; it sustains life's duration in time, and when it ceases the whole creature is dead. Here again the Hebrew concept is notably different from the Greek idea of a transient *pneuma*, which is just the vitalizing principle infused temporarily in a body.

Hayyim

The implication of *hayyim* is qualitative as well as sustaining. The true human life is one of "length of days" and "good days" of peace and joy before Yahweh, lived in faithfulness to the divine Law. Attached to the commandment of Moses to honor father and mother, there is a promise, not a threat: "that your days may be prolonged, and that it may go well with you, in the land which the Lord your God gives you" (Deut. 5:16). It is interesting to note that the customary philosophical distinction between one's natural-physical life and the life of the soul cannot be found in this biblical view. To be alive means to experience the fullness of the unity of flesh and spirit, body and soul.

Dam

The idea that life is infused into a body may seem to have been indicated in the Hebrew attitude toward *dam*, blood. The blood obviously flows through the body; it thus seems to be the carrier or vehicle of something precious, namely the power of life. This was a most common belief in ancient cultures, accounting for varieties of sacrificial rituals involving the offering of flesh and blood for the propitiating of just or vengeful deities. In the rite of slaughtering a bull, the *taurobolium*, devotees of the earth-goddess Cybele stood beneath the grill of the altar and believed that the bath of blood gave them new life. Between enemies there is "bad blood," but a compact of "blood brothers" is made by the mingling of wounds on clasped hands. Prejudices of racial superiority have always been bolstered by the belief that lesser breeds and races had inferior blood, while thoroughbred persons were "full-blooded." The examples are numerous, drawn from cultic practice, superstition, colloquial expression, and developing physiology. Following Jewish sacrificial tradition, the Christian Letter to the Hebrews adduces much evidence to show that the new covenant was ratified and sealed by the shedding of the "precious blood" of Jesus as the self-immolating high priest. The hymns and homilies of Christian piety are thus replete with blood imagery. Similarly, Galen, the great physician of the second century, taught that the vital spirit (*pneuma zōtikon*) was carried by the arteries to sustain life, and his theory persisted in Europe for centuries.[18] Wounded in battle, it was said, a warrior's "life-blood ebbed out."

The Hebrew view went further than considering blood to be just the vehicle of life force. The blood *is* the life (Deut. 12:23; Lev. 17:11). *Nēpēš* does not flow through *dam*, but life and blood are the same. "Thus blood stands for the bare life of man."[19] Hence the Levitical injunctions against eating blood, and the abhorrence of spilling it. Hence, too, the consistently monistic anthropology, according to which human life is the totality of physical and spiritual (or soulish) dimensions.

The first clear understanding of how blood flows through the cardiovascular system of the body was not grasped until the sixteenth century by Michael Servetus, and fully described by William Harvey a century later. But the connection between blood and heart was obvious to the earliest observers. The main interest of ancient Greeks was the physiological importance of the heart.

Aristotle was led both by his careful scrutiny and by "a rational inference" to conclude that the heart is "the principle of life and the source of all motion and sensation."[20]

Leb

The Hebrew insight or intuition gave *leb*, the heart, an even more prominent place in the human constitution. The Jewish conception of *leb* was not anatomical but in the main closer to what the Greeks called the mind (*nous*) or reason (*logos*). By actual count the word *leb* is employed 858 times in the Hebrew Bible. Wolff calls it "the most important word in the vocabulary of the Old Testament anthropology."[21] Of course, *leb* conveys a number of meanings of the attributes of life, some of which we still intend, even if only metaphorically, by the word heart: courage, desire, will, affection. But the weight of emphasis falls upon the cognitive, thinking power of *leb*. "We must guard against the false impression that biblical man is determined more by feeling than by reason," warns Wolff.[22] The familiar contrast drawn by Blaise Pascal between reasons of the heart and reasons of the head is a modern, not a biblical, view. The *leb* itself is the place of reason and thus of the distinctly human life that is responsive to Yahweh.

Performative Language

Although there are other words as well, these five Hebrew words—*nēpēs*, *ruah*, *hayyim*, *dam*, and *leb*—are the primary ones employed in the Scriptures to indicate and partially define human life. As C. A. van Peursen observes, the biblical Hebrew is performative rather than descriptive language.[23]

The words pertaining to human life are definitive only in the sense that they are not static, abstract, or categorical definitions. The chief concern of biblical anthropology is with what men and women become, that is, with their redemption or salvation, rather than with classification. Edmond Jacob summarizes:

> The OT has nothing strictly new to say about human nature. No purely scientific interest may be seen. . . . this first emerges under Hellenistic influence. The specific qualities of the God of Israel are what invest biblical anthropology with a distinctive coherence which non-biblical world anthropology does not have.[24]

The three major cultures on the shores of the Mediterranean Sea, from two to three thousand years ago, pursued an understanding of the phenomenon of life, using religious as well as philosophical and primal scientific categories. Hebrew, Greek, and Latin vocabularies were fashioned during this pursuit. Perhaps it was the implicit hope of their thinkers that selection of the appropriate words would mean the grasping of the elusive reality itself—a perennial problem of semantics and epistemology which is ultimately doomed to frustration.

Our comparison of words and nuanced concepts to this point has shown that translatability is not characteristic of every word; and where translation does seem fairly easy it may actually cause deception and misunderstanding. To use the common English word, "soul," in translation obscures the fact that it involves real differences from the correlative Hebrew, Greek, and Latin terms being translated. With a stated caution based on perception of this danger, therefore, we can set down the approximate correlations among the three ancient languages as follows:

HEBREW	GREEK	LATIN	ENGLISH
nēpēs	*psuchē*	*anima*	soul
ruah	*pneuma*	*spiritus*	spirit
hayyim	*bios/zōē*	*vita*	life
dam	*haima*	*sanguis*	blood
basar	*sarx*	*caro*	flesh
	sōma	*corpus*	body
leb	*nous*	*mens*	mind

It is evident by their deficiencies of language that the Hebrews were less interested in physiology and psychology than in the integrity of human beings as moral agents and faithful creatures of Yahweh. Such an analytical enterprise as the contemporary investigation of the mind-body relation would have been quite impossible within the arena of biblical discourse, even apart from the total lack of neurological knowledge.

Two hallmarks of the Hebraic view nevertheless stand out as

uniquely characteristic of human life. The first, as has been emphasized, is the integrated unity of each person. Although the two elements of a dichotomous anthropology are found in the biblical material, the dualism of body and soul is not there. Neither is the trichotomous scheme implicit, as though a person's constituent parts were the body, the spirit, and the mind or soul. Greek and Latin thinking was congenial to the two- or three-dimensional person. But to say any one of these equivalent words in Hebrew is to mean them all together in the unitary man or woman.

The second mark is the relational identity of life as distinct from both the utterly individual or solipsistic conception and from the view of life as implying the mass of the species. Life requires indispensable relations in two directions: to others in the human community and to God. There is, to be sure, a strong sense of individuality. The prophet Jeremiah was sure that Yahweh knew him as an individual before he was born, even before he was conceived: "Now the word of the Lord came to me saying, Before I formed you in the womb I knew you, and before you were born I consecrated you" (Jer. 1:5). The psalmist believed that the divine-human communion began even as he was being shaped by God in his mother's womb: "thou didst knit me together in my mother' womb . . . Thy eyes beheld my unformed substance" (Ps. 139:13–16). The same conviction made Job recognize his human kinship with his servant: "Did not he who made me in the womb make him? And did not one fashion us in the womb?" (Job 31:15).

We note, however, that the personal individuality is conditioned precisely by one's having been created and known by Yahweh, rather than by one's being a member of the species and enjoying a separate existence. Capturing both of these relationships required for personhood—to God and to other humans— T. S. Eliot asked a question and answered it thus:

What life have you in you have not
    life together?
There is no life that is not in
    community.
And no community not lived in praise of God.[25]

Hans-Walter Wolff concludes the matter with this summary explanation:

> Everything that is said about breath and blood in the anthropology of the Old Testament is instruction in the ultimate reverence for life. But this reverence is not derived from the manifestation of life itself; it is based on the fact that the breath and blood belong to Yahweh, and therefore life without a steady bond with him and an ultimate tending towards him is not really life at all.[26]

EACH ONE IN GOD'S IMAGE

The capability for personal relation with both God and other persons is grounded in another basic biblical concept—the image of God. This concept is found in the younger of two traditions of creation, the "Priestly" tradition. "Let us make man in our image," says the Creator, apparently to himself, "in our image, after our likeness; and let them have dominion. . . . So God created man in his own image, in the image of God he created him; male and female he created them" (Gen. 1:26–27). The very familiarity of these simple sentences conceals the three enigmas in them, over which scholars have puzzled and debated for centuries. One perplexity is the difference, if any, between the "image" (*tselem*) and the "likeness" (*demuth*) of God. A second problem is the actual meaning of these two terms, both of which imply visibility with respect to the eternal, invisible God. The third is the rapid sliding between singular and plural nouns and pronouns: "Let *us* make man in *our* image. . . . let *them* have dominion. . . . God created man in *his* own image. . . . *he* created *him*; male and female he created *them*. And God blessed *them*."

Challenging the whole concept of a true creation, of course, is the age-old and ever-popular taunt, reversing the biblical sentence: Man made God in *his* image.

Extended commentaries on these two verses from Genesis, even whole books on just these verses, have not resolved the riddles; so any brief interpretation here is sure to be less than satisfactory. Nevertheless, the doctrine of *imago Dei* is too important for biblical anthropology to be merely mentioned without comment, or worse, omitted altogether from the discussion because of disputes about its meaning.

Two theories about "image" and "likeness" are often cited. First, if the two terms are regarded as referring to two divine attributes, then "image" is the capacity to reason and "likeness" is the original godlike righteousness of Adam and Eve before the Fall from grace. Second, the two terms constitute a rather common Hebrew literary form, the doublet, in which two similar words, repeated for rhythm and emphasis, mean only one thing.

The actual meaning of each term, or of both together, might be one of the following as proposed by various old traditions and modern theologians: erect stature as distinct from animals; authority over the rest of creation; stewardship for creation; a shadowy physical resemblance; the use of self-reflecting reason; free will and moral responsibility; personality; capability of personal relation to God; the complementarity of male and female which is the ground of human community.[27] These are not capricious ideas of pious or literary imagination. Behind each of them is a history of insight and reflection, both religious and philosophical, by which due respect is intended to be paid to human identity and dignity. Not all these renderings are in accord with the biblical belief in the creation of humankind by God. Some imply that the human being is either a divinity or an emanation of divine essence; others suggest a fragmentary mortal reflection of the perfect immortal Mind, Soul, or Reason (*Logos, Sophia*). Such interpretations readily lend themselves to dualistic theories of animated human bodies, or else support the contrary view of pantheism, according to which everything is one with the eternal Reality and there is no discontinuity between God and humanity. The biblical emphasis upon Yahweh as the Creator and humanity as the creature stands opposed to those theories. But, for better or worse, the undefined concept of the "image of God" has been, and remains, a convenient anthropological vessel which can be filled with a variety of disparate ideas. The pitcher of Jerusalem, so to speak, can be filled with deliciously tempting Athenian wine.

One interpretation seems to make sense of the enigmatic mixing of singular and plural nouns and pronouns in the creation story. Why does God become plural and man male and female? Because personal relationship in love belongs to the very being of God, from which human community and love derive. In this view, strongly argued by the Swiss theologian Karl Barth,[28] human beings constitute a parable of the divine nature itself, in the sense that proper or authentic humanity—beyond species identity— requires the complementarity of persons. So the division of sexes is not merely a general provision for reproduction; it enables human beings to know the most intimate I-thou relation, which is that of love. Barth even dares to suggest that the personal relation of complementarity between men and women is eternally prefigured in the communal nature of God, namely, in the mystery of the divine Tri-unity. This is clearly an interpretation of creation refracted through the theological lens of the New Testament. It does not commend itself, then, to Jews or others who judge trinitarian theology to be a subversion of monotheism. However, it was the exemplary Jewish philosopher, Martin Buber, who advanced the attractive belief that the intimacy of the I-thou relationship in human experience is derived from Yahweh.[29] But the idea that essential humanity consists of the complementarity of male and female does not find favor with either the defenders of celibacy or the advocates of feminism. Observation and common sense seem to support the reasons for their dissuasion. Nevertheless, if either Jews or Christians who believe in the givenness of personal relationship in love as an essential of human life look for a clue to the origin of that quality in the biblical doctrine of creation, they will find parabolic, if not literal, veracity in this interpretation.

MADE FOR GOD AND ONE ANOTHER

What is the import of this Hebraic view of life today? Is it credible and acceptable? Is it of use in philosophical biology and bioethics? In brief, is this view true as a coherent indication of the reality we call human life?

It has been asserted above that the theory of psychosomatic unity of the human person is congruent with, and agreeable to, present understandings of human identity. Few people today would argue against the legitimate use of the word "psychosomatic." Its appropriateness in the field of health and medical care is quite evident from the differing standpoints of both psychiatry and physical medicine. The term is literally applicable, however, only where the reality of both *psuchē* (= soul) and *sōma* (= body) is recognized. Where dualism has given way to idealistic monism, as in the practice of Christian Science or spiritual healing, the *sōma* is excluded as mere illusion. Where materialistic monism is accepted, the *psuchē* itself is a myth, which upon scientific examination can be exposed and explained fully in terms of neurology, chemistry, and electrical energy. This latter form of monism, materialistic monism, is obviously more prevalent in Euro-American cultures, where scientific humanism has permeated the intellectual water and atmosphere. Even so, there persists noticeably an unquenchable and unacknowledged vestige of belief in the transcendent soul, or spirit, or just the human consciousness and mind, whether or not attributed to the God of biblical faith. And it is to this sense of psychosomatic life that the unitary anthropology of Hebraic origin pertains and testifies.

Human life is essentially unitary, but also relational. The category of personal relationship, as distinguished from pure individualism and as an indispensable to human existence, also finds favor and usefulness for people who deal with questions of life's value and moral quality. It is well understood that each human being, at whatever state of prenatal or postnatal development, is a unique genotype. Genetic inheritance from two parents who are themselves unique makes of every human being ever conceived an unrepeatable and irreplaceable unit of the race. But this does not mean that each one's life can be defined independently of, or unrelated to, other members of the species. It is not a sufficient statement of the essential attribute of relationship to repeat the formula, "the human being is a social being." Such a formulation can mean only that human individuals tend to be gregarious or that they must live interdependently in order to survive. They have this social trait, which is a necessity, in common with many animals. Nor is the character of human relationship, whether aggressive or altruistic, adequately treated by including the human species under the general category of sociobiology. Edward O.

Wilson defines this new science of sociobiology as "the systematic study of the biological basis of all forms of social behavior, in all kinds of organisms, including man."[30] Wilson declares quite positively that anything and everything which we recognize as human life and behavior is the result of the effect of genes upon cells, tissues, and organs of the body. Does this bold thesis really and fully do justice to the behavior of human beings? This is to be seriously contested. To be sure, man *is* essentially social in a primal, biological sense, even as bees, termites, and zebras are. "To the biologist," writes the reflective scientist Adolf Portmann, "human life also appears primarily as a system" wherein the "individual is structurally correlated with a social organism."[31]

The naive Hebraic insight and the sophisticated generalization of the experimental biologist coincide in noting that human life is by nature social. What should be equally notable and agreeable is the recognition of the uniquely *personal* quality of the relational character of human beings. It is a quality of variable development, form, and intensity—virtually negligible in an unborn child and minimal in a newborn infant or a grossly retarded person. Even so, whether minimal or richly developed, the capacity for personal relationship belongs to the essence of human life, whether that capacity be expressed by physical gesture, touch, look of the eye, or spoken or written word. Personal communion cannot be appropriately equated with the herd, flock, swarm, school, or colony among the rest of the animals. Such human communal ties are not between mere specimens of the species; they are between sisters, brothers, friends, enemies, colleagues, or fellow members. Some animals, to be sure, mainly mammals and birds, demonstrate their innate ability to recognize other individuals of their own or different species. Monogamous "marriages," pair bondings with lasting fidelity, are not uncommon. And pet animals take on aspects of human behavior as they attach themselves emotionally to children, women, and men. In fact, the friendly and even passionate mutuality of human beings and their domesticated or homebred pets provides important data for philosophical anthropology. Many a person testifies to having a closer friendship with horses, dogs, cats, or other so-called dumb brutes than with any human being. People and animals even practice the rudiments of communication with vocal sounds. However, the conscious recognition of human beings for one another, their mutual exchange of self-identities, and the inexhaustible variety of their verbal communications, are of an order categorically different from that of which animals are capable. These too belong to the image of the biblical God, the God who speaks.

If interpersonal community is an aspect of life that fits into modern secular anthropology as well as into the biblical concept, the second direction of relationship is more problematic—that is, the personal communion with Yahweh, or God, or Transcendent Spirit. If life's identity and meaning presuppose a supranatural origin and a Creator who is disposed toward personal relationship with men and women, is a "God-hypothesis" required for the understanding of life? Not if the god so conceived is a speculative abstraction, a *deus ex machina* or "god of the gaps" of human knowledge, or some unknown power which reason requires to account for otherwise inexplicable phenomena. Undoubtedly Grene is correct when she writes of most contemporary biologists: "They have, of course, and rightly, no wish to serve the ends of theology."[32]

But do they serve the ends of *bio*logy by categorically excluding from their thought the very possibility of a transcendent, creative, and personal Reality such as the name God symbolizes? To be sure, there can be no synthesis of materialistic naturalism and theism, no easy harmonizing of ancient biblical literature and modern scientific knowledge. All that the modern proponents of the ancient faith of Israel and Christianity ask is that the *possibility* of its enduring validity in accounting for human life in its fullness be acknowledged. This is where the openness of Portmann's mind, like that of many others in our time, seems most helpful. Although he cannot, as a scientist, discern "the phenomenon of the spiritual" in human life as it is studied empirically, Portmann is prone to say that "the biologist searches for the spirit" without accepting a priori definitions, but is impelled to fill out his understanding of life.[33] This possibility is akin to what the great French mathematician and philosopher Blaise Pascal called "the wager." Pascal was talking of the existence of God, of course:

Let us weigh the gain and the loss of wagering that God exists. Let us estimate these two cases: if you win, you win all; if you lose, you lose nothing. Wager then that he exists, without hesitating.[34]

There is a clear analogy here between wagering on God's existence, or reality, and on the truth of the Hebraic, biblical insight into human life. This is because both the reality of God and the proper concept of what it means to be human are not abstract propositions. They are, rather, the key to the fulfillment of life's given potential. As such, they are well worth the bet.

4

THREE DIMENSIONS OF
ONE LIFE

HEBRAIC ROOTS AND
CHRISTIAN BRANCHES

According to the Hebraic insight, human life in both its essence and existential fullness derives from the divine creativity. It is so conceived in both the physical-biological and the psychic-moral sense. This unified conception, having by now had a history of more than three thousand years, persists as the normative view of contemporary Jews. It has survived the distortions caused by Hellenistic philosophy and the alternative attractions of both modern idealism and materialism; it has assimilated the compelling power of the scientific method of evolutionary biological and anthropological investigation. This also remains the normal Christian understanding of life, despite those same distractions and the aggression of contrary ideas. However numerous and important the differences in theology may be between Judaism and Christianity, they are not to be found in the doctrine of human life and its moral nature. The transition from the Hebrew accounts of the creation and purpose of life in the Old Testament (Hebrew Scriptures) to the Greek Christian concepts in the New Testament was not an abrupt break. The fact that the New Testament was written almost wholly in Greek by no means implies that the early Christians adopted a Hellenistic anthropology in place of the Hebraic. Recent critical studies have generally served to magnify the Jewish character of the New Testament and minimize the Hellenistic, in spite of its language. In fact, the translation of the traditional Hebrew law, prophets, and writings into Greek had been achieved by the famous seventy scholars (thus, the *Septuagint* version) within three centuries before Jesus' birth. Moreover, as one considers the thoroughly Jewish nature of Jesus' own thought, faith, and outlook, as well as the plain fact that the earliest Christians were nearly all Jewish, this easy transition should not be regarded as unusual. It is natural enough to perceive how Christianity took over the ancient Hebrew anthropology. Indeed, given the fact that the doctrine of Christian faith is built primarily upon the person of Jesus of Nazareth, it would have been quite impossible without this Hebraic monism for people to conceive or believe the two cardinal affirmations about him. These two articles of faith in Jesus Christ were and remain radical developments of the religion of Israel; and they were, of course, the ones that soon constituted the wall of belief which still separates Christianity from Judaism. The first is the doctrine of the Incarnation: that the eternal Word (*Logos*) or Son of God assumed human flesh and became a real individuated man named Jesus. The other is the witness of Jesus' resurrection from death. Remove these two doctrines from Christian faith and it becomes an entirely different kind of religious manifestation. Why are both of them considered possible only if the Hebraic insight is true? The reason has been amply demonstrated during recurrent disputes within the church as occasioned by the challenge of Greek dualism.

"The *Logos* became *sarx*—the Word became flesh" (John 1:14). If the premise in Platonism and Stoicism of the radical split between eternal soul and temporal matter were true, the assertion of Incarnation would be absurd, impossible, unthinkable. Just to say that the Logos, as divine Reason, accounted for the unique wisdom and virtue of Jesus would be consistent with Greek philosophy. The Logos could be *in* him as reason. But it could never *become* mortal flesh, a bodily man. Jesus might *seem* to be the God-man, argued devotees of the popular religious movement known as Gnosticism; but his *seeming* (docetic) humanity could hardly be integral with his divine nature. So dangerous was this Gnostic idea in the view of Christians before the end of the second century that the First Letter of John made it the negative test of the true and false "spirits" which claimed divine sanction: "Every spirit which confesses that Jesus Christ has come in the flesh is of God" (1 John 4:2). The writer of this small apostolic letter declared that the witnesses of Jesus as the Incarnate

Logos—called here "the word of life"—had heard him, seen him, touched him with their hands (1:1). As the Christ, Jesus was audible, visible, tangible. About such a statement there is nothing docetic, seeming, or illusory.

The resurrection of the body from death is the second pillar of Christian faith which rests upon the older Hebraic insight. The formula projected by Paul, as he strugged to offer intelligible answers to the doubting questions of Greeks in Corinth, defines the indispensability of this doctrine: "If there is no resurrection of the dead, then Christ has not been raised . . . then our preaching is in vain and your faith is in vain" (1 Cor. 15:13–14). On a rock below the Parthenon in Athens, Paul had once lectured a group of intellectuals, including Stoic and Epicurean philosophers. He had won a sympathetic hearing for his message about Jesus Christ up to the point where he spoke about the resurrection: "Now when they heard of the resurrection of the dead, some mocked, but others said, 'We will hear you again about this' " (Acts 17:32). Those in Greece who had become Christians could hardly avoid being skeptical. Immortality of the soul? Yes, of course. Their whole philosophical and religious heritage affirmed the belief that each soul automatically, without special divine assistance, continues to live in a disembodied state after physical death, or else migrates to another body. This is an idea that is congenial to persons ancient or modern, naive or sophisticated, who are not thoroughly materialistic in their outlook. But resurrection! Of what? The body! The Christian faith affirms this. The crucified Jesus Christ still lives. And we too will be "raised up" to live.

Early Jewish reflections on life after physical death had no place for resurrection. Even immortality was a matter of frank agnosticism. It was enough to affirm the God-given unity and integrity of human beings in the time-bound experiences of their earthly existence. One looks in vain for clear statements or assurances of immortality, eternal life, or resurrection in the older books of the Old Testament. Yahweh is the living Lord of living creatures. When they die, their lives are no more. *Nepēs*, *ruah* and *hayyim* are at an end.

Jewish faith and reasoning were not content with this lack of a concept of the so-called afterlife. The story of Job, written as early as the seventh or as late as the fourth century B.C., expressed the pathetic human question which had to be answered somehow: "But man dies and is laid low; man breathes his last and where is he? . . . If a man die, shall he live again?" (Job 14:10, 14). The answer to the anguished cry came late, but it came with strength. The basis of hope for the whole person's survival of death was not found in the inherent worth of the individual human being alone, but primarily in the will of Yahweh to fulfill his promise of the final triumph of his righteousness and his redemptive purpose for Israel and humankind. The prophets announced their eschatological vision of "the day of the Lord." "He will swallow up death for ever," said Isaiah (25:8). "Thy dead shall live, their bodies shall rise," he announced (26:19). The Hebrew yearning for unending personal communication with Yahweh, expressed with poignant faith in the many psalms, could not be confined by a hopeless, melancholy concession to final mortality. Since God's truth, righteousness, and mercy must "endure to all generations," the death of faithful and righteous men and women cannot be regarded as final. The eternal law of the Lord must triumph, if not during this temporal life, then afterwards. By the time of the compiling of the apocalyptic Book of Daniel in the second century B.C., the belief in resurrection was widely and firmly established. But here resurrection was not a guaranteed beatific immortality; rather it was, as all of life is, conditional upon faithfulness to God's moral law: "And many of those who sleep in the dust of the earth shall awake, some to everlasting life, and some to shame and everlasting contempt" (Dan. 12:2). As a modern Jewish theologian expressed this belief, resurrection means "not a disembodied soul that has sloughed off the body, but the whole man— body, soul and spirit joined in an indissoluble unity."[1]

The faith of the New Testament, then, did not invent belief in the resurrection from death to life. The Pharisees in Jesus' own lifetime, always depicted as his adversaries, were nevertheless convinced of the resurrection about which he spoke. Probably they would welcome his vision of the separation of the good sheep from the evil goats at the expected judgment (Matt. 25:32ff.). What was new, shocking and incredible—but constitutive for

Christianity—was the testimony of the women and the apostles to the resurrection of Jesus himself. In other words, early Christians were claiming that the great event which some of the Jews believed would eventually happen "on the day of the Lord," in either a far-off future or even in a time-beyond-time, had actually happened to Jesus in Jerusalem. And it was one of the Pharisees, the apostle Paul (Phil. 3:5), who more than any other person succeeded in interpreting Jesus' resurrection to Jews and Gentiles as the key to life's purpose.

IN HIM WAS LIFE

The first feature common to both the incarnation and the resurrection is their basis in Hebraic anthropology; that was the thought-form, premise, or presupposition about life that made these alleged events credible and intelligible to people. There is a second bond, however, namely the Christian belief that the mystic power of human life itself was present in Jesus and conveyed to others by these two events.

Of the eternal Logos who became flesh it was written, "In him was life and the life was the light of men" (John 1:4). In the crucified Jesus who was raised from a genuine death Paul perceived the decisive meaning for all humanity: "For as in Adam all die, so in Christ shall all be made alive" (1 Cor. 15:22). Higher ascriptions than these can hardly be conceived. The very essence of human vitality as derived from the Creator is attributed to Jesus Christ.

What can be said about such a claim? Various responses are easy to hear. "Sheer fantasy! Nonsense!" says a skeptic. "Where is empirical evidence?" demands a scientist. A scholar of religions observes, "Hyperbole not unusual among enthusiastic religious devotees." "Typical Christian arrogance," says another. "What do those words about life really mean when heard by believers and nonbelievers?" asks a philosopher. Or a mystic might murmur, "You will not find the meaning until the meaning finds you."

Even in circles of the most exacting critical research and reflection, it is conceded that the natural phenomenon of organic life is a deep mystery, and that human life is mystery of the profoundest depth. So it is not to be expected that theological statements about life should be less mystery-shrouded, or more readily explicated, than scientific ones.

The primary question to ask is the one which keeps arising today—whether there is an impassable gulf between scientific and theological discourse about life. Are they referring to two absolutely different realities: theology to spiritual, eternal life; science to the psychophysical earthly and temporal life? If so, we must abandon at the outset any hope to bring them into dialogue or conjunction or meaning. This may indeed be the judgment of critical thinkers who do not necessarily despise either theology or science but who delineate two utterly disparate fields of inquiry. They may see in this dichotomy either two dimensions of the concept of human life, or else two distinct referents of the word "life." One is the palpable, describable, and measurable life of a functioning vascular system, growing and deteriorating tissues, electrical brain waves, reproductive capacity, activity, sleeping, and inevitable death. The other is the life of imagination, fantasy, self-consciousness, evaluation, prayer, love, and aspiration. According to the unitary anthropology, the two dimensions of the one life are kept together. They are conjoined within an individual person and also in a generalized view of all human life. This unity cannot be maintained where there is perceived to be a hostile, centrifugal bipolarity of spirit and matter in thinking about life. Movements of thought toward both horizons of the dualistic span, toward the "east" of idealism and the "west" of materialism, eventually result in the choice of either one or the other.

The life that Christian faith professes to see revealed and embodied in Jesus Christ, and conveyed by him, includes more than the purely ideal or spiritual dimension. It is not a moral quality or a spiritual sensitivity added to the natural physical life, as polychrome decoration was added to statues of bare wood. In his own ministry and teaching, Jesus was concerned as much with people's bodily health and well-being as with the state of their souls. In fact, he apparently was more widely known and followed for his healing touch than for his prophetic and inspiring words. Knowing the basic needs of living, he was concerned that the hungry be fed and the oppressed be freed for fruitful and rewarding life on earth. Yet, as he insisted, life is more than food and clothing and shelter. Having the essentials, you should not be anxious about them (Matt. 6:25). But life is also suffering, frustration, and tragedy as well as righteousness, love, and joy in the presence of God, who is good and faithful; and life is hope for the resurrection of eternal life.

Jesus' own anthropology, then, was clearly and typically Jewish. It included, with undifferentiated attribution to God, three dimensions at once: the bodily life of the flesh, the psychic and moral life of the soul, and the fulfilled and resurrected life of the complete person. All three of these aspects of life are lived in personal relationship to God and to a community of persons.

The three dimensions of the one human life, which are implicit in Hebraic anthropology and manifest in Jesus' acts and words, become explicit in several books in the New Testament. As suggested earlier, neither the dualism of soul and body nor the triadic scheme of body, mind, and spirit is an appropriate formula for the biblical understanding. "Older distinctions between dichotomy and trichotomy must be abandoned so far as Old Testament anthropology is concerned," judges Edmond Jacob. "Man is always seen in his totality, which is quickened by a unitary life."[2] The Hellenization of biblical religion is well illustrated by the familiar triangular symbol of the YMCA, sporting the motto "body, mind and spirit." The Greek words which correspond to the symbol—*sōma*, *nous*, and *pneuma*—are not the ones used for "life" in the Bible, except in 1 Thess. 5:23 where the biblical uniqueness of their conjunction is conspicuous.

If death had removed Jesus permanently from further recognition by his friends and followers, his teaching would probably not have been long remembered for its novelty and power, and his healing acts and personal tragedy only a bit longer. But Christianity from the start has been the religion of Easter. The prominence of Mary Magdalene in history has been greatly enhanced by artists and writers who gladly represented her as a somewhat erotic figure in the otherwise unromantic stories. But her real importance, according to one tradition, is that she was the first person to be able to declare, "I have seen the Lord!" (John 20:18). In the evening of the same Easter day the disciples of Jesus could also say to their doubting colleague Thomas, "We have seen the Lord" (John 20:25). And Jesus' appearances to larger numbers, even to "five hundred brethren at one time," are recorded in the earlier tradition of Paul (1 Cor. 15:6). Trying to explain this to an excited, curious, but skeptical Jewish public, the apostle Peter appealed to Psalm 16, attributed to King David (Acts 2:24):

> For thou dost not give me up to Sheol
> or let thy godly one see the Pit. (Ps. 16:10)

It was not possible, said Peter, for death to confine Jesus. Why not? In terms of the developing Christology which resulted from Christians' reflection upon this staggering event, mortality as the power of decay, corruption, and nonbeing could not prevail over the insuppressible surge of life in the man who brought the creative power of God to earth. As Christian liturgies, hymns, and iconography have been shaped to express this decisive mystery, Jesus' resurrection was a cosmic victory over finitude and evil; he desolated the gates of hell; by death he trampled down death.

Considered critically, there is much here that is poetry and imagery. The symbols are archetypal and the language metaphorical. How else is it possible to speak of such an event? The theme of dying and rising is ancient and broad in religious mythology, often linked in fertility cults to the vernal restoration of vegetation after the "death" of winter. As for death, it has been the preoccupation of many religions and has been apostrophized by countless poets: "Oh, Death . . ." Apart from religion and poetry, we speak with grim humor of "cheating death" or suggest that "death takes a holiday," implying that death has its own character and power. In the New Testament and traditional Christian language, death is also considered a lethal power and is virtually personified. Death is the antithesis of life, the "last enemy" over which Jesus has triumphed in behalf of all persons. Though many "cultured despisers" of Christianity are content to toss the belief in Jesus' resurrection into the same trash bag with similar myths and legends, this belief persists in the minds of recognizably sensible people. Indeed, it is the very basis of their faith to believe that this event truly happened, at a definite time, at a certain place, and with real people telling about it.

Is the resurrection the same as a physiological resuscitation? Christian faith and theology emphasize most strongly that the two are utterly different, even though many people with a genuinely pious attitude ignore the difference. Modern medical technique has made resuscitation commonplace, especially within a few minutes of cardiac arrest. In face of the danger of drowning, most sailors and young campers are taught the method of mouth-to-mouth resuscitation. Hospital technology is so dependable that resuscitation is usually a mere matter of choice, determined by the probable extent of damage to the patient's brain inflicted by the loss of oxygen over an elapsed time. This raises some severe questions about the wisdom and moral rectitude of those who make the decision, questions that depend for answers upon one's concept of human life itself. But they did not apply to the case of the dead Jesus.

As the creeds had to declare, against charges that Jesus' death was not real: he was crucified "under Pontius Pilate," was dead, and buried. Resurrection defies phenomenal explanation, though efforts have been made to make it just as intelligible as resuscitation. Some have gone so far as to propose that a scientific account of the resurrection can now be given in terms of particle physics and molecular biology; that is, Jesus' supernal mind was able to control the atomic and molecular action of the cells of his body. Thus, he consciously "decomposed" himself in the stone-sealed tomb and then reconstituted himself outside.[3] Like all other theories that tell how Jesus returned to the land of the living, this most recent and allegedly scientific theory avoids the clear implication—which for a critical mind is inevitable—that Jesus would either die a second time eventually or else retain his physical, material body indefinitely. Resurrection does not permit such questions. It means, rather, that the whole person of Jesus was raised from death to a wholly new order or dimension of life.

THREE GREEK WORDS

The Greek language is renowned for its store of nuanced words, as well as for the constructibility of compound words from its root-terms, prefixes, and suffixes. Our constantly expanding technical and scientific vocabulary is thus derived largely from Greek. The old saying is justified: "The Greeks had a word for it." Like the classical language from which it descended, the common, or koine, Greek in which the New Testament was written possessed words of subtly shaded meanings. For lack of such variety, modern European languages must often translate them inadequately or even inaccurately. The word "love" is a well-known example. English, German, French, and Italian are equally at a loss to provide equivalent terms for the three Greek terms, *erōs, philia,* and *agapē.* "Love," *die Liebe, l'amour,* and *l'amore* carry the baggage of too many connotations—romantic, aesthetic, sexual, greedy—to express the distinctions which, in Greek, are approximately equal to "desire or lust," "friendship," and "self-giving love." The forms of Latin *caritas,* favored in Catholic translations, unfortunately convey today an attitude of patronizing condescension toward the object of love.

Translating "life" from Greek presents the same kind of problem. What that word means to a person depends upon his or her cultural conditioning, education, bias, or belief. Also, the meaning of "life" varies according to the different contexts in which the term is used, and the adjectives used to modify it. The semantic variations in the possible uses of "life" seem almost limitless. Yet, in making an English version of the New Testament it has been unavoidable and necessary in many instances to employ this one word as a translation for three Greek terms—*bios, psuchē,* and *zōē.* These three terms have had histories of changing meanings in ancient usage; but they acquired, or even were given, particular senses by the Christian biblical writers.[4] An extended analysis of the three can illumine the meaning of "life" for Christian faith and understanding as well as for wider secular thought.

Bios

Due to the numerous and familiar English derivatives from *bios,* it might well be assumed that this was the primary word for "life" in the common Greek of the New Testament. The Greek root is known widely today in such terms as "biology," "biosphere," "biopsy," "biographic," "bionic," "bioethics," and "antibiotics." Advertising agencies find it convenient to use *bios* in coining trade names for new cosmetic and pharmaceutical products. Virtually without exception, medical terminology is based upon *bios* wherever "life" is intended.

These direct derivations from *bios* in its classical usage are understandable in view of the immense influence Aristotle's scientific philosophy has had for two millennia. In his writing *bios* was the prominent word for life. For example, in the *Nicomachean Ethics*, ruminating on the essentials of a good human *bios*, Aristotle finds three types of life, graded in value: the pleasurable, the political, and the contemplative.[5] The most evident expression of life is in the seeking of happiness or pleasure, which for "the mass of mankind," who are "slavish in their tastes," means "preferring a life suitable to beasts." The political life is a superior dimension in terms of virtue, since it aims at honor and higher virtue. Beyond that is the happiest kind of *bios*, which is the life of contemplation by use of reason. Aristotle writes: "the life according to reason is best and pleasantest, since reason more than anything else *is* man."[6]

In the New Testament, however, *bios* is more notable for the paucity of its uses than for its prominence. In the few places where it appears it does not refer to the physiological or sentient life of animals or the differing dimensions of human life. It is never used as the designation for human life in its full realization. Instead, *bios* usually indicates the mode, or manner, of living one's life: bare subsistence, survival, the means of keeping alive. The examples are familiar ones: When Jesus commended the poor widow for giving two copper coins to the temple treasury, it was because they were a good share of her *bios*, her simple means of staying alive (Mark 12:44). In Jesus' parable of the prodigal son, the inheritance which the younger son received and squandered was his "living," his *bios* (Luke 15:12–30). Similarly, in English ecclesiastical parlance, a "living" was the endowed parish church that guaranteed at least minimal sustenance to a clergyman, also appropriately called his "benefice." In another parable, the Word of God was sown like seed on different kinds of ground and soil; but the cares and pleasures of *bios* choked the young plant as weeds do (Luke 8:14). This word also carries a pejorative connotation, where life is equated with lusts of the flesh (1 Pet. 4:2), pride of life (1 John 2:16), and the trivial affairs of life (2 Tim. 2:4). Only in 1 Tim. 2:2, where *bios* is commended as "quiet, peaceful . . . godly and respectful in every way," does it mean a normal kind of life. This is as close as the New Testament literature comes to using *bios* in the positive sense of a physically healthy and morally commendable or satisfying life. *Bios* is in other places either descriptive of the manner of keeping alive, or else indicative of a morally reprehensible mode of living.

The adjective *biotikos* emphasizes further this reduced estimate of life as conveyed by *bios*. In the two places where it appears (Luke 21:34 and 1 Cor. 6:4), *biotikos* refers to the ordinary affairs of daily living rather than to the power of vitality or the excellence of life. It bears no resemblance, therefore, to the modern medical term "antibiotic," which as a negative term is concerned with the varieties of cellular life that are inimical to human health.

Now, the ordinary means of staying alive and the common affairs of daily life, or even the perversions and corruptions of normative human good, are not less than human life. But qualitatively and morally considered, they are the least of the three dimensions of life as these are discerned in the biblical terms. From the level of human existence that is indicated by *bios* our analysis is drawn upward by the connotations of the word *psuchē*.

Psuchē

More frequently used than *bios* and of richer substance in the New Testament is *psuchē*. Because it is a common word in languages other than Greek, easily transliterated into "psyche," most people no doubt consider it to mean simply the "soul" or perhaps "mind," which in unity with the body constitutes the life of an individual human being. Such is the definition of the Oxford Dictionary, which presupposes a dualistic, or dichotomous, anthropology in which the psyche and the body, though united in life, are separable by death. This is the same antithesis which we found to be so easily but wrongly assumed to exist between the Hebrew *nēpēs* and *basar.*

There are some traces of such dualism in the New Testament; or at least the lexicon of life—soul, mind, spirit, flesh, body—serves to suggest the dualistic concept. But the fact that the unitary view prevails overwhelmingly is illustrated by the Bible's deliberate refusal to regard *psuchē* as a mere component of *bios,* life. *Bios* and *psuchē* are both words for life, but not as parts of the whole. They are two dimensions of the one phenomenon of human life, of which there is a third, *zōē,* still to be discussed.

There are two peculiarities about the meaning of the English words derived from *psuchē.* The first is the present loss of the sense of a real soul in the very field of inquiry that makes the greatest use of the technical words built upon this root, namely, psychology. Whether one who is psychotic or psychopathic seeks psychotherapy by a psychoanalyst or psychiatrist, the chances are very slight that any persons involved in the case will think or talk about a *soul* in distress. It is more likely that the person's ego, self, or personality will be discussed, in close relation to neurobiology and all the environmental factors that shape the psyche. John Hick is no doubt right in observing that the "soul" has become, for a great many people today, only a "valuing name for the self . . . [connoting] the moral and spiritual personality," but not referring to an aspect of life which has come from a transcendent or divine source.[7]

The other odd thing is that in modern English parlance the psyche does not mean life as such, as *psuchē* quite frequently does in the New Testament. Once again it is noted that the unavoidable dependence upon the one word "life" makes it most difficult for readers of English translations to appreciate the biblical nuances. A comparison of various modern versions reveals how biblical translators have struggled with this problem—with varying degrees of success.

The earliest and simplest meaning of *psuchē* was that of drawing breath—hence the breath of life. But the New Testament expresses developed meanings that are more sophisticated than that both psychologically and theologically. These meanings can be classified as referring to three aspects of life: (1) the objective reality of mortal life as normally lived; (2) the subjective center of the living self; and (3) the enduring life that still needs salvation for transcending mortality and sin.[8]

The Objective Reality of Mortal Life

There is a conventional, common-sense way of speaking of life that requires no divine revelation or even intellectual acumen for discerning differing dimensions, states, or values of living. The plain reference is to a human being's vital functioning and experiencing, the obvious alternative to which is death. For this elemental concept the New Testament uses almost without exception the noun *psuchē*. (The verb form cannot be employed to say "she lives" or "to live" for the curious reason that the verb *psuchō* has the meaning "to make cool." It is used just once: "And because wickedness is multiplied," predicted Jesus of the coming apocalyptic days, "most men's love will grow cold" [Matt. 24:12]. When a verb for "live" is needed, it is *zaō*, of which the distinctive noun *zōē* is a form.)

Psuchē designates the life that is put at risk by the courage to face menacing dangers and destructive forces. King Herod had tried, by ordering the slaughter of all male infants in Bethlehem, to end the *psuchē* of the baby Jesus (Matt. 2:20). Preaching on the mountain, Jesus urged his followers not to be overly anxious about *psuchē* (Matt. 6:25). Indeed, he insisted upon the hard challenge that to be his loyal disciple could mean, not only cessation of such anxiety, but even coming "to hate" one's *psuchē*, when concern for it constitutes a barrier to faithfulness (Luke 14:26). In accord with this injunction, Paul the Apostle could honestly declare that, in comparison to the mission for Christ, "I do not account my *psuchē* of any value nor as precious to myself" (Acts 20:24). So he and his partner, Barnabas, were described as "men who have risked their *psuchas* [pl.] for the sake of our Lord Jesus Christ" (Acts 15:26). In this willingness to expose themselves to death as martyrs to faith, early Christians were guided and inspired by the singular example of Jesus himself. He had said about his own mission in life that it is the purpose and destiny of the Son of Man "to give his *psuchē* as a ransom for many" (Matt. 20:28; Mark 10:45). In John's Gospel, where "life" is usually expressed by *zōē*, Jesus three times utters the promise that, like a faithful shepherd, he will lay down his *psuchē* for the protection of his sheep (John 10:11, 15, 17). And he makes of this resolute intention a general criterion of the love (*agapē*) he teaches: "Greater love has no man than this, that a man lay down his *psuchē* for his friends" (John 15:13). In none of these instances would it make sense to employ *bios* as "manner of living" as previously described. Neither would it be acceptable to translate *psuchē* as soul, lest this imply a separable distinction from the body. *Psuchē* means the person's whole life that is sacrificed; but it does not indicate the full intrinsic worth or human character of that life, nor does it refer to the manner, or mode, of living it. Rather than being a general term for the phenomenon of life, it is always referring to a person's concrete existence.[9]

The Subjective Center of the Living Self

The subjective reality of life is additionally meant by *psuchē*. It is in this dimension that the biblical anthropology seems capable of being more comfortably discussed in terms of modern psychology. Quite clearly the biblical writers use the word to designate three aspects of the person's inner life: the mind/intellect, the will/volition, and the affective senses/feeling or emotion. These are not neatly delineated categories. Thoughts, desires, and sensory responses are intercausative and interreactive. Not one by itself, nor all three together, can be said to constitute the whole of life; yet all are essential to the wholeness of life. So each is called *psuchē*.

"My *psuchē* magnifies the Lord," exclaimed Mary in anticipation of her child's birth (Luke 1:46). But the elderly sage, Simeon, in the temple, warned her that "a sword will pierce through" her *psuchē* because of the tragedy of her son's life (Luke 2:35).

To God himself is attributed a subjective center of being. This is indicated by the citation of Isa. 42:1 in Matthew's Gospel (12:18), where Jesus is identified as the chosen Servant of the Lord, in whom Yahweh's soul (*psuchē* = *nēpēs*) "is well pleased."

The commandment to love God "with all your *psuchē*" is asserted by Jesus in summing up the Torah; but the Greek version of this primary command includes three other terms which are likewise associated with one's *psuchē*—all your heart, strength, and mind (Luke 10:27; Mark 12:30; Matt. 22:37; cf. Deut. 6:5). There is thus a fourfold emphasis upon the sincerity of trusting love, since real distinctions cannot be drawn between heart and strength or mind and soul.

In fact, *psuchē* is translated as "heart" in some passages where the ideas of "heartily," "whole-hearted," and "heartening" (encouraging) are intended (Acts 14:22; Eph. 6:6; Col 3:23; Heb. 12:3). Or, where the "heart" is broken in sorrow (as in Mary's case) it is written of Jesus himself that he approached his experience of suffering and death with a *psuchē* that was "very sorrowful" and "troubled" (Matt. 26:28; John 12:27).

Then there are places where the meaning of *psuchē* can only be one's mind, with emphasis upon cognition, thought, and attitude. Paul urges the Christians of Philippi in Greece to be "of one *psuchē*" (Phil. 1:27), but in Iconium in Asia Minor the adversaries of Paul stirred up and poisoned the *psuchas* (pl.) of the Gentiles so they would not listen to his preaching (Acts 14:2).

Human Life as a Transcending Reality

Just as *psuchē* is the center of one's inner life in a spatial, temporal, and psychological sense, it is also the center of human life as a transcending reality. Life goes beyond this mundane, sensate experience of it. Materialists who do not believe in transcendence could use *psuchē* in the two ways already described, but not in this third way.

In the biblical view each human life with its personal identity is considered transcendent in two aspects. One is its personal relation of communion with God, receiving and responding to the divine acts of communication and endowment of gifts and powers. The other aspect is the inherent but potential capacity to enjoy the saving grace of God not only during earthly life but also in the resurrection, or re-creation, to eternal life. As Eduard Schweizer puts it, *psuchē* is "the life which is given to man by

God and which through man's attitude toward God receives its character as either mortal or eternal,'' Schweizer further notes: ''We never read of *psuchē aiōnios* or *athanatos* (eternal or immortal) but only of the *psuchē* which is given by God and kept by Him to *zōē aiōnios* (eternal life).''[10]

Given the pervasive influence of Platonic thought in both Christianity and Western philosophy, it is tempting to think that it is really Plato who is speaking through the evangelists and apostles about *psuchē* as the immortal soul. But this is a deceptive idea. The soul as such is definitely not immortal. Matthew makes this utterly clear when he reports an admonition of Jesus that is strange and perplexing to a mind conditioned and informed by idealism: ''Do not fear those who kill the body but cannot kill the soul'' (Matt. 10:28). *Psuchē* here must be soul rather than life, since life and the body (*sōma*) cannot be distinguished and separated in this way. But is this not dualism? we are prone to ask. Is Jesus a Platonist? No; for he continues: ''Rather fear him who can destroy both soul and body in hell.'' Who is the one who has that total power of annihilating a life? Another human being? No. A despotic, satanic adversary, contending against God the Creator? No; that would imply a cosmic dualism in which God was the weaker power. Jesus does not say that God is the destroyer, in the sense of the capricious Hindu god Shiva. But as Creator of the whole life of a person, meaning the unity of *psuchē* and *sōma*, God alone has the power of uncreating the life he created, if such were his will. As Karl Barth comments, this passage of Matthew ''does not say that the soul cannot be killed, but only that no man can kill it, while God has the power to cause both soul and body to pass away and be destroyed in the nether world. Hence we do not have here a doctrine of the immortality of the soul. . . . the *psuchē* is the whole man, the life of his body, he himself as he exists in this bodily life.''[11]

A most emphatic exposition of *psuchē* as the life of transcendent value is found in Jesus' powerful aphorism about losing and saving one's life, and in the rhetorical question about wealth:

For whoever would save his *psuchē* will lose it; and whoever loses his *psuchē* for my sake and the gospel's will save it.
For what does it profit a man to gain the whole world and forfeit

his *psuchē*? For what can a man give in return for his *psuchē*? (Mark 8:35–36; Matt. 10:39; 16:25–26; Luke 9:24–25)

The English scholars who were appointed by King James to produce the authorized translation of 1611 may have been thinking more in Hellenistic than Hebraic terms when they translated *psuchē* in the aphorisms as "life" and in the rhetorical questions as "soul." One can gain the whole world but in so doing lose what is the most precious part of the person, the soul. This choice of language seems to indicate a dualism of life and soul in which the soul is the transcendent value. Modern translators of the Revised Standard Version (1946) instead chose the word "life" for their formulation of these questions involving use of the term *psuchē*. So it is life as such that is the most precious value. Life can easily be lost by anxious striving for self-interested fulfillment which dissuades a person from discipleship; but life is found and saved in the acts of faithfulness and love that Jesus and the gospel require.

Does *psuchē* in the aphorisms have two meanings? Scholars are of divided opinion, and the division makes a significant difference. Some interpret Jesus' sayings as a distinction between two kinds of life: to lose the earthly life and gain the eternal or heavenly; or else, to lose the ordinary human life and save the true self and personality.[12] Such interpretations commend themselves to our minds if we prefer to think dualistically; and for many, this is the reasonable, common-sense way of accepting Jesus' paradoxical assertion. As a matter of fact, it will be shown that John's Gospel decisively modified this traditional statement of Jesus in just such a way—so that disregard, or even hatred, for one's life (*psuchē*) is rewarded by the transposition to eternal life (*zōē*) (John 12:25) But here in Mark's Gospel, according to the well-argued analysis of Gerhard Dautzenberg, Jesus is not talking in such terms. Holding to the practical, personal, historical meaning of *psuchē*, as a Hebraic concept, Dautzenberg prefers to speak of it in the modern sense of existence. Jesus' strong admonition is then heard as a blunt warning to the disciples, who were in jeopardy because of their faithfulness to him in a dangerous situation. They were setting out on foot to Jerusalem where hostile religious and political powers awaited Jesus and his band. He did not promise them as reward a higher quality of life or eternal salvation. Rather, he encouraged them to stand by him in the coming danger in Jerusalem by saying that they would survive it. Jesus, then, does not distinguish two kinds of existence, the earthly and the heavenly, between which one can choose; human existence is fundamentally unitary and indivisible. And for the disciples, this means commitment of life to following Jesus.[13]

It is in the two short letters attributed by tradition to the apostle Peter, especially the first, that English translators have preferred to delineate *psuchē* as soul in each of the following passages:

" . . . the salvation of your souls." (1 Pet. 1:9)
"Having purified your souls . . . " (1:22)
" . . . the passions of flesh . . . war against your soul." (2:11)
Christ is " . . . the Shepherd and Guardian of your souls." (2:25)
" . . . entrust their souls to a faithful creator." (4:19)

Surely these phrases seem to suggest a dualistic anthropology. Schweizer calls 1 Pet. 2:11 "the most strongly Hellenized *psuchē* passage in the New Testament."[14] This would appear to be consistent, though, with the general emphasis of the letter (which is possibly based on a sermon of instruction and exhortation at the time of baptism). The focus of its teaching is upon a life of strict restraint and discipline for Christians who are suffering as "aliens and exiles" in a world from which deliverance is anticipated. Under such circumstances it is not unusual to think of the suffering human body as something distinct from, and subordinate to, the indomitable soul. Nevertheless, this is not necessarily the case in 1 Peter. In each instance *psuchē* could in fact be rendered "life" as well as "soul." Then life would mean a person's potential transcendence of time and mortality through the faith in divine grace and power. According to Hebraic Christian thought, then, a person or self as a whole life would be purified, guarded, and saved.

The Distinction Between
Psuchē *and* Bios

The New Testament is not unique, but it is unusually consistent, in expressing the nature of human being and experience of

101

life by the word *psuchē*. It would be fatuous, of course, to suppose that the many persons responsible for the Greek books and letters—collators of tradition, writers, redactors—had agreed on a common usage as a matter of theological, or anthropological, principle. Reasons militating against such a supposition are self-evident. The New Testament had no editor. Even so, whether by design or chance, it is apparent to us today that the dimension of life as *psuchē* is different from that called *bios*.

Can the distinction of the two dimensions be seen and described in modern parlance? Does it have pertinence to differing kinds of existence today? Yes. We can say that *bios* is *mere* life, lived on a level of bare subsistence. Many exist at such extremity of hunger or exhaustion that sheer survival can be their only concern. Many others are in the throes of incurable disease or debilitating physical or mental illness. *Bios* refers to biological, physical life; but from the Christian perspective it is nonetheless a creation and donation of God. *Bios* may thus apply also to human life as yet unborn, still dependent entirely upon the physiology of the mother. Or *bios* is life in infancy, before the minimal requisites of personhood have appeared, such as self-consciousness, mutual recognition of others, communication, and the rudiments of speech. For persons who are mature and not suffering disability of ill health, their manner of living may be so thoroughly dominated by sensate satisfactions that they can be said to be living virtually in the dimension of the *bios*. In the ontological sense, then, *bios* refers to life that is genuinely human, but it is life that, qualitatively evaluated, lacks the attributes which would mark the realization of its potential humanity. This is what the biblical usage of *bios* suggests for our understanding today, even though such considerations are not explicitly expressed. They can be extrapolated to fit diverse conditions of life and living.

Moving to those many instances in which life and its components are referred to in the New Testament by the word *psuchē*, clearly distinguished from *bios*, we may infer a second dimension of life, also describable in contemporary language. This is what people think of as ordinary, or everyday, life. It is at least the experience of existence of all persons who do not live on the outer margins of sanity, consciousness, health, or vitality. *Psuchē* too is life created and endowed by God; but, compared to *bios*, its possibilities and potentialities have been, or are being, more highly realized. This does not mean only a higher level of happiness, however, since sorrow and tragedy are also an inescapable portion of life. So living in the dimension of *psuchē* may include the joys of proximate fulfillment: health, education, work, family, love, social relations, recreation, and causes for hope in the future. Contrariwise, *psuchē* may be a life of great difficulty, sorrow, and tragedy, marked by constant struggle to overcome poor health and relative poverty; to withstand unjust discrimination, political oppression, and even humiliating incarceration; to endure loneliness and resist pessimism and cynicism. In either case, whether comfortable and happy or difficult and frustrating, *psuchē* is psychophysical human life in which needs beyond those of bare survival are satisfied.

Psuchē is the dimension in which the majority of human beings live at any given moment. But it is an unstable state of life. Many remain in it until death. Others slip gradually, or fall suddenly, into the dimension of *bios* because of accident, illness, senescence, tragic decision, or inadvertent misfortune. *Psuchē* is thus the life for which one can be thankful to God (some might say luck) and which one endeavors to live responsibly, creatively, and well. It is the life that can be deliberately thrown away by the atrophying effect of sloth, by careless dissolution of morality, or even by despair and suicide. *Psuchē* can be lived in any society or culture without meriting the acclamation of any particular achievement, grandeur, or heroism. Contrary to the advice Jesus gave, one can be extremely anxious about preserving and enhancing one's *psuchē*. Such self-concern and self-serving are in fact the dominant motivations of millions of people. But, for those who have been grasped by the power of altruism or love for another, or by moral commitment to a great cause, it is not inconceivable that life itself can be sacrificed.

"Is not the *psuchē* more than food?" demanded Jesus (Matt. 6:25). What is that "more"? To be quite literal, there is a great deal needed in life and for life besides food—needed even by those who commend the simple life. A late letter of the New Testament exalts the simple life: "for we brought nothing into the world and we cannot take anything out of the world"—true enough!—"but if we have food and clothing, with these we shall be content" (1 Tim. 6:8). It then describes the peril of desiring to be rich and so being captivated by "the love of money [which] is the root of all evils" (1 Tim. 6:10). In these words are some implicit assumptions about life—not about the manner of life only, which is *bios*, but about the very nature of it. One assumption is a divine bias in favor of austerity and against inordinate wealth; for it is the drive of acquisitiveness leading to wealth, or sustaining wealth, which inevitably causes the corrupt and hurtful uses of the power over others which is a concomitant of wealth. No consideration is given in the letter to the possibility of a person's being charitable, humble, and magnanimous while also being rich; for this is seen as a contradiction in the understanding of life. The second assumption follows upon the first: the kind of life (not just behavior) which is the alternative to that of sensate and materialistic acquisitiveness is one of compliance and conformity with the divinely favored style or pattern, including "righteousness, godliness, faith, love, steadfastness, gentleness" which are the marks of "eternal life" (6:11–12). The writer (probably not Paul) urges people to "take hold of the eternal life to which you were called when you made the good confession," adding that even the rich, by eschewing greed in favor of others, "may take hold of the life which is life indeed" (6:12, 19).

The life that is *indeed* life, real life, true life is, in the New Testament, *zōē*. This is the third of the three dimensions of the one human life.

Zōē

The differences among the three dimensions of life are indeed qualitative. There are not three kinds of human life, if by that formulation we mean three things that are *essentially* different. The Hebraic unity holds not for just the body and soul of an individual but also for the general phenomenon of all human life. Just as there are no individuals without bodies (disembodied souls) and no individuals without souls (soulless bodies), so there is no human life that is without the human identity.

People often make statements to the contrary, applying one of the two kinds of dualism. The first dualism, as often noted and criticized, separates body and soul. The second dualism, as too seldom noticed, separates human life from the subhuman, or barely human. According to the latter distinction, many individuals never quite rise above the critical line of humanhood either before or after birth; and many, even before death, fall below that critical line. Of what does the line consist?[15] And who is competent to draw it across the vast demographic ledger of the human race? The delineation of that line—if it be at all defensible—depends upon the definition of "human" as such. And the competence of anyone to draw that line is a corollary of the arrogance of those who believe their definition to be legitimate.

The New Testament's use of $z\bar{o}\bar{e}$ certainly reinforces a concept of "quality of life" (if we may risk the inclusion here of that indeterminate and slippery phrase). With perhaps one exception, however, the New Testament never teaches that a life without quality is worse than no life at all. The only suggestion of a "wrongful birth" in the modern legal sense is not given as a statement of general principle but as a rhetorical emphasis laid upon the implications of the traitorous act of Judas Iscariot in a unique situation: "For the Son of man goes, as it is written of him, but woe to that man by whom the Son of man is betrayed! It would have been better for that man if he had not been born." (Mark 14:21). Just as it is never asserted that no life is better than some kinds of life, neither is it assumed that anyone's life is ever without a certain quality, and hence of value as an object of God's love.

What New Testament thought and diction do convey with clarity is a pattern of ascending realization of the purpose for which one was created. What is that purpose? In one sentence it can be summed up in a saying attributed by John's Gospel to Jesus: "I came that they may have life [$z\bar{o}\bar{e}$] and have it abundantly [*perisson*]" (John 10:10). A better rendering of the Greek adverb would be "in full abundance," meaning the realization in experience of the plenitude of life. That statement, of course, is widely known and often uncritically used in expressions of piety. But it still begs the question: What do "fullness" and "abundance"

105

actually mean? Such words are like empty vessels: they symbolize a certain carrying capacity but are themselves in need of being filled.

Thus, the word *zōē* has a potential for meaning, a carrying capacity that the thought of the earliest Christians was quite able to fill. It cannot be said that the rich meaning of an abundant, fulfilled, and eternal life was already inherent or implicit in *zōē* when the biblical writers began to employ it. In fact, as the study by Bultmann has revealed, the secular and common (koine) Greek usage of the noun carried no specialized freight of meaning; it was synonymous with *bios* in the vocabulary of Greek-speaking Jews, such as Philo of Alexandria, who was contemporary with Jesus and the first Christians.[16]

Other than modern Greek, the modern European languages, notably English with its eclectic disposition to borrow from Greek, have made almost no use of *zōē*. Even familiar English words such as "zoology" have only an indirect lineage by way of *zōon*, meaning animal. As a curiosity, there was a nineteenth-century toy called a zoetrope, and this name has been given to a Hollywood film studio. Also, two companies making, respectively, insecticides (!) and vitamins, have appropriated *zōē* for their trade names. As for the woman's given name Zoë, it was first favored in the imperial Byzantine court where it bore the connotation of endearment and a man would praise his loved one as "My life." In short, as compared to *bios* and *psuchē*, this little word *zōē* has made hardly any contribution to modern vocabulary.

This dearth of derivatives would scarcely seem worth noting except for the significant meaning with which *zōē* was invested by New Testament Christianity. Just why the word has suffered neglect in subsequent Christian literature is only a matter of conjecture. Also conjecturally, this lack may account for the inadequacy of any Christian theology or doctrine of human life as such, for relatively little has come down to us from historical tradition. Yet, there it is in the Bible—most prominently in the Fourth Gospel and the letters of John where *zōē* can justly be called the key word of faith. Furthermore, it is used with singularly important meanings in Paul's letters and the three Synoptic Gospels. In most cases, *zōē* refers to a person's life made abundantly full—hence of eternal quality. In these instances, *zōē* is inseparable from Jesus Christ and faith in him. He is the source from which life derives and is given, the power that sustains and directs it, and the goal toward which it leads.

There is no validity in the insistence that one's credulous acceptance of this neglected word *zōē* can suddenly give a person a new vitality and purpose in living. That would be an artificial and spurious kind of verbal inspiration. A word in any language can be a powerful means for evoking emotional and moral response; and *zōē* could conceivably have such power if it were fully understood and accepted by a large community of people. Even so, we must avoid any romanticizing of the word or exaggerating its inherent power as it appears in the New Testament or is appropriated by an individual. The vital power is not in the three-letter word. The power is in the God to whom the word points and the means by which God conveys the power of life to us human beings. Lacking specific words to express these meanings, we could quite reasonably coin two new ones to facilitate this whole discussion of life's meaning and value according to the biblical insight. "Zoetic" would refer particularly to the qualitative aspect of life, and "zoethics" would designate the systematic inquiry into life's ethical implications.

It is notable and strange that the writers of the four Gospels as well as Paul give to the verb form *zaō* a diversity of meanings that the noun *zōē* does not express. This is no doubt due in part, as we mentioned above, to the fact that *zaō* serves as the active verb form of both the nouns *psuchē* and *zōē*. Therefore, what may be regarded as the ordinary, commonplace nature of life and living as denoted by *psuchē* is also expressed by *zaō*, rather than by *psuchō*, which is the cognate, albeit inoperative, verb form of *psuchē*. That is to say, *zaō* serves to express the colloquial "live one's life," whether the life indicated is one of ordinary existence (*psuchē*) or of particular moral and spiritual quality (*zōē*). "To live," in the sense of *psuchē*, can mean just to be alive rather than dead, to recover vital health after illness, to live "in the flesh," or to live "by bread alone."[17]

When the verb *zaō* implies the life of *zōē*, however, there is a manifest heightening of quality and spiritual value. "To live," in the sense of zōē, means to enjoy personal existence according to the power and grace of God, to have life in the Spirit, to live in Christ, and to have eternal life.

This discussion of Greek words is just so much academic, etymological pedantry if it does not contribute to our personal quest to learn what life's meaning, the meaning of *our* life, can be today. Persons who regard the Bible as, at least, a unique source of human knowledge, or the channel by which divine revelation is conveyed, will not consider our question put to the biblical texts as of merely literary or historical interest. The question is truly existential: What do the texts say about *my* life *now* and of its potentialities? The literary, historical question would only be: What did the earliest Christians mean by professing that "Christ is our life" or saying of the eternal but incarnate Logos, "in him was life"? Today's existential question, more concretely put, is: How is my life dependent for both existence and quality upon that divine reality or power which early Christians first experienced and discerned through faith in Jesus Christ? Or, anyone seriously interested in hearing a reply might ask: What more of life's meaning can there be for me in acknowledging and believing Jesus Christ than I can know without him? Fair enough. Unless positive and concretely personal answers to these existential, and sometimes anguished, questions can be provided, the claims made by Christians about Jesus Christ are apparently empty. Indeed, the whole system of Christianity, the church and its mission ultimately depend upon this question, since for humanity life and its meaning are the ultimate matter.

One of the earliest examples of Christian preaching is the speech which the evangelist Luke received from oral tradition and included in his primary history known as The Acts of the Apostles. The apostle Peter spoke to a crowd of people in Jerusalem, amazed because they had seen an act of healing in the name of Jesus Christ. Rather bitterly he declared: "But you denied the Holy and Righteous One, and asked for a murderer to be granted to you, and killed the Author (*Archēgos*) of life, whom God raised from the dead" (Acts 3:14–15). Whatever Peter's Aramaic or Hebrew word may have been, the Greek *Archēgos* was a remarkable title to be applied to Jesus so soon after the crucifixion event in that city. Translators into English have had differing ideas of what it means. The old King James Version says "Prince of life," a noble but inexact rendering. The "Author of life" is better (Revised Standard Version); but more literal and significant is "him who has led the way to life" (New English Bible). Clearly the intended message is that Jesus, who was crucified and raised from death, has some critical importance for the very reality of life which all people share.

A further stage of defining Jesus' relation to human life was established by Paul when he wrote to the Christians at Corinth about the mystery of the resurrection (1 Cor. 15:35–58). Here he contrasts the creation of Adam with the raising of Jesus, both of which were creative acts of God.

> The first man Adam became a living being [*psuchē*]; the last Adam became a life-giving [*zōopoioun*] spirit. (15:45)

As expected, reasonable comparison might have been made by Paul if he wrote that Jesus had been re-created from the dust of the earth, from his dead body, just as Adam had been. However, the unexpected, staggering assertion is the ascription of life-making power to Jesus. Thus, the one who is made alive, raised up as "the first of those who have fallen asleep" (1 Cor. 15:20), is himself the one who makes alive. Jesus is both the subject of vivification and its object. Here is shown the very nexus of his divinity and humanity, sharply distinguishing him from other prevalent exemplars of how the power of life is present to human experience.

Jesus is not, on one hand, the cosmic, heavenly, vitalistic force, or the principle of life, which pervades everything that lives, moves, and grows. He is neither the numinously animistic power of primitive religions, the entelechy of Aristotle's biology, the cosmic *atman* of Hinduism, the disembodied immortal soul of Neoplatonism nor divine emanation of Gnosticism. From Jesus' own lifetime in Galilee until today, people have devised schemes to identify him with one or another of these religious types or philosophical concepts. But one thing stands in the way of such identification: the Incarnation, the becoming human of the eternal

Logos, the Son of God. Only by becoming really human could he really die a mortal's death and receive life.

On the other hand, Jesus was not just a charismatic holy man, a religious genius, clairvoyant seer, righteous prophet, or perceptive teacher, whose ultimate talent was to offer guidelines to the achievement, through morality or mysticism, of a higher level of life and living. Only by being one with God could he really, rather than metaphorically, be the *zōopoioun*, the life-maker, "who abolished death and brought life (*zōē*) and immortality through the gospel" (2 Tim. 1:10).

The implications of this faith for human experience were brought out most prolifically by the Gospel of John decades later than Paul's letters and the other three Gospels of the first century. The keynote of *zōē* is sounded in the opening paragraph. And Jesus' whole ministry and purpose are summed up at the closing of the book: " . . . that believing you may have *zōē* in his name" (20:31).

In the hymnic form of the prologue, the foundation stone of John's theological edifice is laid: the eternal Logos, the Word, is the creative power of God: "All things were made through him" (1:3). Next to that premise is laid the second stone: "In him was *zōē*." (1:4). The third is the incarnation: "And the Word became flesh and dwelt among us" (1:14).

If this structure of thought is not to be vitiated by spiritualizing, allegorizing, or relegating it to mythology, the three premises must be accepted for what they say. The eternal Word is God exercising the unconditioned power of creativity; the creation is materially real; the life of the Word is conveyed to the creatures; and the Word dwelt among us as Jesus Christ.

In verses 3 and 4 of the prologue, the absence of punctuation in ancient Greek texts has allowed two variant translations. Jerome and Augustine noted this in the fifth century and saw the possible differences of meaning, as have other translators and commentators to the present time.

The first form is more familiar to English readers who know the King James and the Revised Standard versions: " . . . without him was not anything that was made. In him was life, and the life was the light of men." This reading separates the rest of creation from the reference to human life, which alone comes from the Word.

The second form broadens the extent of giving the Word's *zōē* to all living creatures, and is not only "the light of men." Following Augustine's Latin ("*Quod factum est, in eo vita erat*")[18] the Revised Standard Version offers his version in a footnote as an alternate: " . . . was not anything that was made. That which has been made was life in him." Recent scholars have been inclined to prefer this form, which is textually acceptable, because it conveys an important meaning about the creation of life which is fully consonant with John's theology. In an awkward but literal way Bultmann proposes: "What has come to be in him (Logos) was the life."[19] More smoothly, the New English Bible paraphrases slightly: "All that came to be was alive with his life."

The difference in meaning between these two is subtle, not readily perceived on first reading, and largely a difference of emphasis. The former implies for human beings the moral and spiritual dimension as well as the exemplary character of the life of the Word, that is, of Jesus Christ. The incarnate Word, as the true light of the divine will and wisdom, reveals what life should be. Life should be, and can be, eternal (*aiōnios*) for those who have faith or are in communion with God through love. John never ascribes eternal life to God or to the Word, of course, because it is the divine life that defines the eternal quality rather than possesses it. So the purpose of the coming of Jesus Christ is to make available to persons the abundance or fullness of life as it is in accord with God's loving intention. And the condition for receiving the gift of eternal life, as Jesus reiterates in this gospel, is believing in him as the Word or Son whom God has sent for this purpose.

It is not said in the prologue that the presence of Jesus is the first and the only opportunity for people to obtain *zōē* in its fully eternal quality. Later in the gospel, the matter of believing in Jesus becomes the categorical requisite for receiving it; and the theological problems of particularism and exclusivism have become acutely difficult for our modern mentality. So far as the Jews of the first century were concerned, C. H. Dodd's study shows that the Jewish expectation of everlasting life in the eschatological Age to Come agreed entirely with John's presentation of the life that Jesus offers.[20] However, the reference to "darkness" (v. 5) and the people's rejection of the Word (v. 11) imply the dreadful consequences of willfully living apart from, or in opposition to, the Word of life. The sense of this first reading of 1:4 is well summed up by the Catholic scholar Rudolf Schnackenburg:

> The Logos, too, in our hymn is to fill men with the divinely spiritual life which is in keeping with their being, the life which distinguished them from the rest of creation [non-rational] and consists both of knowledge of their god-like nature and of a blessed union with God in holiness of conduct. This divine life-giving force was fully present in the Logos, as in an inexhaustible source, fed from the depths of the divine life.[21]

So, the manner of living one's *zōē* is empowered by the Word.

The emphasis of the latter reading is upon the divine power that creates the *zōē*, rather than upon the life as lived. The incarnate Word does more than reveal, illuminate, or even offer and convey *zōē* to persons. He creates and makes life of eternal quality because he *is* life. Here the language of the prologue anticipates a number of decisive affirmations in the remainder of John's Gospel and letters, notable among them being the following:

> I am the living bread which came down from heaven . . . for the life of the world. (6:51)
> I am the resurrection and the life. (11:25)
> I am the way, the truth and the life. (14:6)
> Because I live, you will live. (14:19)

The attributions of these "I am" sayings to Jesus (always a difficult problem for critical biblical study)[22] is fully harmonious with John's other indicators of the vivifying power of Jesus as the divine Son who, as *zōopoioun*, only carries out the creative work of God the Father.

> For as the Father raises the dead and gives them life, so also the Son gives life to whom he will. . . . For as the Father has life in himself, so he has granted the Son also to have life in himself. (5:21, 26)

What might be styled the highly "zoetic" character of John's presentation of Jesus as the source, power, and consummator of *zōē* is also in agreement with the earlier testimony of Paul and the writers of the later letters of the New Testament. As frequently and significantly noted, life for Paul's faith and thought is really equated with Jesus Christ, who since his being raised from the dead continues to live in his body, the church.

For to me to live is Christ . . . (Phil. 1:21)
It is no longer I who live, but Christ who lives in me. (Gal. 2:20)
Your life is hid with Christ in God. When Christ who is our life appears, you will also appear with him, in glory. (Col. 3:3–4)

The dialectic of dualism, which has pervaded this whole discussion of life—equally in science, philosophy, and theology—appears again in the matter of interpreting the New Testament's affirmation about *zōē* in Christ. In the writings of Paul and John there are clear evidences of dualistic thought, though the extent of its influence is a matter of scholarly dispute. That is to say, contrasts are drawn between the archetypal metaphors of light and darkness, eternity and world (*kosmos*), spirit and flesh, life and death. These lend themselves readily to dualistic interpretations of what the Christian faith means about life's nature and destiny. Neoplatonism and even Gnosticism seem to have had such influence upon Paul and John, according to some commentators, that Jesus is considered to have been not human at all, but a divine or semidivine intermediary between God and the fallen world. There is a vast literature on this subject; and it must be admitted that the dualistic world view did penetrate the essentially Hebrew cosmology and anthropology of the New Testament.[23] Into that scholarly thicket we cannot enter here.

One aspect of dualism is critically important for an understanding of how Christian teaching about life can have a practical bearing upon our contemporary concerns for human nature, personal existence, ethics, bioethics, and the biological sciences—that is the dualism that separates the natural, physical life of humans from eternal life. Assuming as a matter of faith that there is reality in the biblical promises of eternal life, must we read the Fourth Gospel with only eternity in mind? Scholars generally agree that *zōē* and *zōē aiōnios* are equivalents when used by John. And certainly in the rest of the New Testament the connotation of *zōē* is that it differs from *psuchē* in a qualitative sense, even though the expression *zōē aiōnios* is mainly confined to the Fourth Gospel.

A statement which is unique in the New Testament makes clear the distinction between *psuchē* and *zōē*. Strangely enough, only a few commentators seem to have noted its importance. This is John's version of the familiar aphorism of Jesus, discussed above, about saving and losing one's life. In the versions of Matt. 16:25 (also 10:39); Mark 8:35; and Luke 17:33 (also 9:24); the life that is both lost and saved is *psuchē*. But John 12:25 effects what appears to have been a deliberate transposition of life's key, as in a musical score: "He who loves his *psuchē* loses it, and he who hates his *psuchē* in this world will keep it for life eternal (*zōēn aiōnion*)."

The differing literary contexts of this saying indicate a reason for this remarkable change. In the three other Gospels, the setting is dramatic and dangerous. Jesus and his disciples are going to Jerusalem, where they expect to encounter perilous hostility. So the context in Matthew and Luke is given a still more intensified color of crisis by Jesus' predictions of expected apocalyptic happenings "on the day when the Son of Man is revealed" and God's kingdom breaks into history. It will be like the flood in Noah's time, or the fiery destruction of Sodom and Gomorrah. To this setting the scene in John's Gospel stands in bold contrast. Jesus and his disciples have already entered Jerusalem with a popular procession. Now Jesus speaks calmly and metaphorically ("the grain of wheat") about his impending death and glorification. Considered in this context, one who by faith does not cling tenaciously to the ordinary dimensions of living (*psuchē*) will be open to the possibilities of higher qualitative dimensions of life as *zōē*, even to eternity.

The fact that *zōē* refers beyond the future to a postmundane, posttemporal life can hardly be disputed. But whether it refers to this inconceivable condition as the exclusive meaning is definitely in dispute. The internal evidence of John's Gospel is neither explicit nor consistent enough to permit an interpretation of eternal life which satisfies all the experts.

One of them, Franz Mussner, holds to the view of *zōē* that "in no single place does it mean the earthly-physical life of men."[24] When Jesus "makes life," it means that he revivifies those who may be called *spiritually* dead; and ultimately in the coming aeon those who have died physically will be raised by the one who said, "I am the resurrection and the life." Seeming to concur with Mussner's stringent interpretation is Raymond E. Brown, who writes that in John's writing "*zōē* never means natural life because only *psuchē* is used for that life to which death is a terminus."[25] The logic of this position is that a person who has received eternal life has already made that transposition that completely removes one from mortal to eternal life. In Paul's language, then, the new creation is really discontinuous with the old. Persons who in faith "die with Christ in Baptism" and are raised with him by the Holy Spirit to the new life (Rom. 6:3–4) are then removed from history. *Zōē* displaces *psuchē* completely.

This exclusive understanding of eternal life still leaves open the possibility of two consequent interpretations. One is that *zōē aiōnios* begins (if one can say that eternity *begins*), or better, that a person enters eternal life only after physical death. The other belief is that eternal life does finally displace *bios* and *psuchē* at death, but that *zōē* begins already in this mortal life in a preliminary, anticipatory way, with the person's attitude of faith in Jesus Christ; but it will not be realized or experienced (whatever that can mean) until after physical death and resurrection. If either of these two ways of viewing eternal life in relation to our temporal life is what the Gospel of John intended to present as Jesus' teaching, or as revelation of the divine truth in Jesus, it leaves present-day believers with a sense of lack.

What is lacking is a clear assurance that the *zōē* which is in the divine Word can be conveyed to us and experienced by us now in our own time. Surely, the whole New Testament message of Jesus, of his interpreters and the early church points to the "last" or "ultimate" realities of God's Age to Come; but just as surely, it speaks of present experience of the redemptive, re-creating power of God in this mortal life. The counterpoint of "now" and "not yet" is played throughout the New Testament. And the "not yet" of fulfillment is already affecting the "now." All the descriptions and promises of eternal life—such as the peace (*shalom*) of God, empowering of the Holy Spirit, new creation, the triadic virtues of faith, hope, and love—indicate the validity of the testimony of the anonymous writer of the Letter to the Hebrews:

> Those who have once been enlightened, who have tasted the heavenly gift, and have become partakers of the Holy Spirit, and have tasted the goodness of the word of God and the powers of the age to come. (Heb. 6:4–5)

The paradoxical relation of Jesus Christ to life in all its dimensions is acutely perceived by C. F. D. Moule in a precise statement which merits reflection:

> Are we being told . . . that it is through Jesus, and through him alone, that *all* the gifts of life are given, *physical* as well as spiritual? When the source of supply for material gifts seems to be cut off, in such a way as to bring home man's helplessness and dependence, it is Jesus who renews the supply. But he does it by drawing upon the supra-material, divine sources of supply by perfect union of will with his Father. . . . The two levels of existence are somehow run together; the normal is transcendentally bestowed, the transcendental is bestowed by one who shares man's mortal life. Indeed, it is because the Word became flesh and dwelt among us that the distinction between the physical and the spiritual is blurred and the two become bewilderingly interlocked.[26]

Rudolf Bultmann, though of a much different theological mind from Moule's, also stresses the duality of both the present moment and the eternal life in John's presentation of *zōē*.[27]

It is by no means a banality to assert that the biblically based faith offers a fulfilled life within this mortal time frame as well as in eternity. We may assume with justification that *zōē* as presented in John's Gospel is neither eccentric nor unique in the New Testament. It is congruent with the hopeful invitation to life's enhancement which is extended to all persons, whether this be designated redemption, reconciliation, peace, salvation, re-creation, or being conformed to the image of God in Christ. Implicit in all these designations is the active work of God by spiritual presence in the world, in history, in the human community, and in each person. Without that faith in divine immanence, there is little to say on the subject.

It will be objected—by some mildly, by others strenuously—that this is an unacceptably restrictive view of the enhanced or fulfilled or even eternal life. It is too religious, too pious, too sectarian, and too Christian. As such, they say, *zōē* can have no meaning for people who, for whatever cause, do not share this faith. What about the humane virtues, the commendable morality, the mental and practical achievements, the spiritual sensitivity that women and men and children by the millions have manifested apart from religions in general and Christianity in particular?

There is indeed a secular, humanistic idea of grace which is noted in the spheres of human relations, ethics, and aesthetics. Some are content to see life's fulfillment in the grace of human love, the grace of a good will, or the grace of beauty. But the theological idea of divine grace does not contradict these; it just presupposes that the source of such gifts and graces as constitute the fully human life is found in God, whether or not the person knows or believes this.

Eternal life does not come as a matter of natural necessity, nor is it earned or achieved by moral effort or striving. It is available to everyone in principle but requires an attitude of receptivity, which is the disposition of faith. The pivotal belief in Christianity is that *zōē* is mediated through Jesus Christ to all. Moreover, *zōē* is not an individualistic experience or possession but communal in nature.

The Greek words *bios*, *psuchē*, and *zōē* as used in the Bible are not three distinct kinds of life; they are three dimensions of quality of the one human life. Clear lines of division between them are not discernible with precision. Their distinctions are not like darkness and light, but like dusk and dawn. We can recognize when we are dealing with any one of the three. However—and this must be underscored—of none of them can it be said that life is not worth living. The constant, intrinsic value of human life belongs to all because God creates and bestows it. In the biological sense, all are *human*, whatever the conditions may be from womb to tomb. By these terms we cannot speak of a developing of life's value, first ascending and then descending, from *bios* to *bios*. The words tell of differing levels of the realization of life's potential, not of its intrinsic worth. Life's meaning and purpose, then, are to outgrow or overcome *bios*, make optimum use of the opportunities of *psuchē*, and keep open and receptive to the fulfillment of *zōē*.

5

A WORKABLE DEFINITION
OF LIFE

Rational choices and decisions of an ethical nature are made on the basis of previously defined concepts. Intuitive choices are not. Two different choices by two persons may be quite rational, but their difference is due to contrary concepts or premises concerning the ethical question at hand. Much depends upon the adequacy and truth of the premises if moral deliberation is to lead to a good decision. This rule is especially pertinent with respect to issues that directly affect the well-being, life, or death of a human being. Such issues keep arising in medical practice, legislation, litigation, and jurisprudence; also in scientific research, industry, and marketing; as well as in domestic relations, procreation, and caring for babies and children. Whatever the question may be—whether technological control of procreation, treatment of unborn and newborn babies, genetic intervention, allocation of resources necessary to life, suicide, penology, "heroic" treatment to prolong one's life when recovery of health seems hopeless, legislating or serving on a jury in regard to capital offenses—in all cases the persons who decide must have a workable concept of what constitutes human life.

How can a workable definition of human life be formulated on the basis of the three sets of knowledge that have been considered in the preceding chapters? These three are: the data collected by the whole, massive investigation of thousands of biological and anthropological scientists; the philosophical concepts shaped by intellectual reflection upon these data; and the religious insights defined by the large believing community over the centuries through the experiences of life lived in communion with God. Many people are content to limit their thought to either the first, second, or third of these sets. Those who are not satisfied with constricting their grasp of life's reality to the results of scientific research are disposed to look also to the philosophers for illuminating interpretations of such results. Still others assume, as a matter of faith and mental commitment, that the full truth about life's nature can be known only from the revelation that God the Creator of life imparts—however interesting and useful the scientific and philosophical material may be.

Any one, or any combination, of the three is a legitimate area for study and intellectual concern on the part of men and women who thirst for more knowledge and crave it for its own sake. But the pressure of the demand for committing one's mind to one or another of these is proportionate to the degree of moral concern one has for respecting, protecting, enhancing, and fulfilling human life. Then it becomes clear that one's theoretical concept, or definition, of human life really is important as the presupposition for making ethical decisions that affect life. And the urgency of that pressure has been, and is being, intensified in the most recent three decades by the rapid development of technical devices for producing, manipulating, controlling, benefiting, and destroying lives.

The preceding analysis of biblical insights on life reveals no general principle of a mysterious animating and directing force that might give a facile religious answer to the perennial debate over mechanism and vitalism. A faith in God, who is creative, personal, and concerned with human history, cannot avoid being antithetical to a mechanistic, materialistic view of life. But the biblical teachings do not speak directly and explicitly against materialism, no doubt because such thinking had no currency in the Semitic milieu from which the Bible came; and apparently it was not a problem needing debate among the Hellenistic people who were converted to Christian faith. The constant concern of the people of Israel and of the early Christians was not with materialism, but rather with the relation between the one God and all human beings.

The Bible contains no discussion of philosophical biology. Despite its many references to particular flowers, birds, and mammals, it is not a book about biology. It expresses a general belief that the one and only divine Creator has made all forms of living creatures, both animal and vegetable; that the beasts and the first human beings are closely related because they were made on the same "day" of creation; that God put whales in the oceans, crocodiles in the rivers, and taught all birds and beasts how to find food and shelter. All living things, according to Psalm 148, thus join in praising their Maker. Had there been in ancient times any knowledge of unicellular life, molecules of DNA, and genes, it is conceivable that the psalmist might have praised God for them and even had them, in turn, praising God along with all other forms of life. All such ascriptions of creative omnipotence, however, are intended only to exalt and glorify God as God, rather than to express wonder and adulation toward the natural phenomena of life as such. Even less congenial to biblical faith than the worship of life as such is the idea of pantheism, according to which all reverence and gratitude for the natural world are tantamount to praise of the immanent deity which inhabits and pervades all nature but does not transcend it.

A Christian concept of life, suggested plainly in the Bible and refined by theologians, is general enough to include the whole range of phenomena of living organisms understood in light of modern biological knowledge under the doctrine of creation. Yet, the Christian view is specific in giving the highest estimate and valuation to *human* life. From the standpoint of religious faith, all living organisms are extremely important, because in their sheer variety, the millions of species and the incomprehensibility of their numbers, they bear witness to the intelligence and power of the Creator. Beyond their cause for reverent wonder, however, the living organisms quite evidently constitute in large measure the environment for the human species, which is preeminent on earth. Although properly numbered among the vertebrates, mammals, and primates, we specimens of Homo sapiens are not "just another" species, nor just the most highly developed in respect to the neural systems. Our uniqueness in intelligence and consciousness, and indeed in physical form, places us in a distinct category which transcends all others. Arrogant as this assertion may seem to some people today, and in recognition of the fruitful advances made lately by scientific investigation of the mental capacities of such animals as chimpanzees and dolphins, it can still be made with confidence.

The human distinctiveness accounts, likewise, for the human dominion over other living creatures as well as the responsible trust to treat all the others with due respect and care. Within the most recent century, more than ever before, human beings have been proving themselves to be the caretakers of the earth and its living denizens. We know of no such reciprocal attitude on the part of other animals and organisms to care for us. What we call ecological or environmental stewardship is a unilateral disposition from our side. However flagrantly we humans have scorned and violated this attitude—and our record is surely horrendous—the moral concept of stewardship remains both a guide to our actions and a judgment against our infractions.

Why is there a restraining idea of stewardship at all? Is it just a prudent device of natural or even genetic origin, by which human survival is best guaranteed? Perhaps we are coming to understand the need for responsibility more thoroughly than ever before in history because of the recently discovered ecosystems; that is, the integral relation, mutual dependence, and symbiosis of many species can be skewed with disastrous consequences by injuring or killing the organisms that are indispensable to a system. This new ecological knowledge provides scientific support for the insight already adumbrated in biblical wisdom concerning human supremacy over all life forms as well as human responsibility for the whole environment.

According to biblical view there is neither need nor cause to be evasive or apologetic about holding an anthropocentric concept of life. The focal point of divine creativity and purpose is humanity. Physicochemical bases of genetic and cellular life are positively acknowledged; but they do not warrant, much less necessitate, a mechanistic, materialistic theory of life. Directing powers in the growth and lifespan of all species and specimens, including humans, operate according to patterns or "laws" intrinsic to the created world. But such powers do not warrant, much less necessitate, a vitalistic biology. The insight and knowledge gained in faith and informed by the Bible, and further interpreted by philosophers and theologians, presuppose that all living entities are derived from God's creation.

Human beings conform to the patterns of cellular growth which are largely explained in terms of body chemistry. In this respect, humans are one with the animals, and most similar to the mammals and other primates. Nevertheless, humans enjoy a unique, inimitable existence with high consciousness, self-reflective purpose, and singular spiritual relation to the divine Creator. This poses a problem. How can something belong to a large general class and yet be in a category distinct and apart from all other parts which make up that class? We human beings are members of certain broad groupings: chordates, mammals, primates. That fact, as designated according to the accepted taxonomic scheme, is undisputed. And certain scientists and philosophers are content today to leave us there among the other animals in our particular slot. "To give preference to the life of a being simply because it is a member of our species," writes Peter Singer, "would put us in the same position as racists."[1] According to his utilitarian concept of life, it is consciousness, not the human species as such, that constitutes value. It is just here, where a commitment to value is at stake, that the importance of the human distinctiveness is found.

When people who work in the general field of the life sciences try to understand what life is, they are limited (as we saw early in chapter 2) to the description and analysis of what can be observed by the eye or detected and measured by prodigiously sensitive instruments. As with all other organisms, human bodies and their overt actions can be minutely analyzed; their neurological responses and psychological behavior patterns can be meticulously traced. Together these comprise the signs of life of the body. But when attention is focused on these bodily phenomena of human life, two other dimensions are unavoidable—the meaning of life and the value of life. These belong primarily to the realm of philosophy and theology, but they are as essential as physiology to the study of life. Indeed, many people claim them to be of greater importance.

A workable concept of human life, therefore, must consist of three parts, answering the questions, what life *is*, what it *means*, and what gives it *value*. The following outline of such a concept is intended to state what is essential in each of these three, and to exhibit an internal consistency of thought about life. The components of the defined concept are presented in the form of theses or short statements. Some require little explanation or discussion; others, much more.

WHAT *IS* HUMAN LIFE?

1. *Human life is but one manifestation of the general phenomenon of life, that is, of the vital energy which animates the cells and tissues of all living things and beings in contrast to their final inertness and death.*

2. *Human life is animal and mammalian, appearing as organic and somatic, that is, in bodily form; it continues itself in a virtually endless continuum through procreation, whereby life itself does not begin again but is transmitted.*

Here there is coincidence and agreement between the biological and theological perceptions. This excludes the purely spiritualized, dualistic idea; it emphasizes the psychosomatic reality. Life is embodied in the biological organism, not as a transient soul striving to escape, but as the expression of the unitary person. This is an idea that many people can accept today, whether or not they are attracted to a biblical, theological anthropology. To those who are neither thoroughgoing materialists nor dualists, it makes common sense to say that soul and body are one. But what happens to that unified personal life when at last the slow, entropic process of dying, or a sudden illness or accident, leads to the event of death? Here, common sense, influenced by intuitive attitudes accruing over long eras of cultural conditioning, provides two opposing answers. One is a reversion to dualism: the physical organism dies and the eternal soul flies away. The other is a reversion to materialism: the physical body dies and decomposes; and since there is no empirical evidence for what happens to the soul, it must die, too. Of course, some have claimed that they experienced a manifestation of disembodied soul in accidental or clinical situations when the heart and lungs stopped functioning for a short time before being reactivated. During the interval between the first critical stage of dying and the resuscitation, as they have later testified, they continued in a conscious but immaterial state, knowing their whereabouts and being aware of people, even while experiencing a new dimension of existence.[2] Opinions about the credibility and veracity of such testimonies are severely divided. Until one is fully persuaded of their verifiability or nonverifiability, it is reasonable to keep one's mind open and one's judgment suspended, even as with other reports of parapsychological experiences and psychic wonders.

What can be said about psychosomatic life in Christian understanding, which differs from both dualism and materialism? How can a unitary life continue after physiological death and still be called embodied life? The Christian understanding can make sense only if the body is defined simultaneously as the physical organism and the complete person. "There is a spiritual body," explains the apostle Paul, that succeeds the physical body (1 Cor. 15:44–46). It is the body of resurrection, the "glorified body," of the new creation. It still retains the personal individuality of each human being after the disintegration of the biological organism.

To assert so unexceptionable an observation as that human life is animal and somatic does not contradict the biblical concept; but it expresses only the first part of it. The physical embodiment, taking shape at first in a fertilized ovum and continuing until the cessation of organic functions, is preliminary to the spiritual embodiment, the idea and expectation of which is patently a matter of faith and hope.

The statement that human life does not begin but is transmitted refers to the life of the human species, not of the individual. In the event of fertilization and the process of earliest multiplying of the embryo's cells, life is popularly said to begin. It is obvious, however, that what begins in this much-debated "moment of conception" is not life as such. It is, rather, the development of a new and genetically unique individual human entity. The furious debate over the question When does life begin? could be softened or avoided if people of both antagonistic convictions would just agree that it is human value, not life, that is being contested.

3. *Individual human beings share in the general character and continuity of the species Homo sapiens; each one has a unique and irreplaceable identity of genotype and, after attaining it, of personhood.*

Each one's uniqueness might be compared to the remarkable individuality of snowflakes, roses, or domesticated animals. But it would be only a matter of curiosity or mild interest if no more than one's genetic makeup (genotype) or general appearance (phenotype) were considered. To be sure, the basis and cause of human individuation are the countless genes, or more precisely, the differing ways the genes are arranged within each long DNA molecule. The greater the number of genes, the more numerous the kinds of variable characteristics in an individual specimen of humanity. In the human species the numbers of possible variables at any time are literally too great to comprehend. The mathematical possibilities of variation can be appreciated if one thinks of the fact that as many as fifty thousand characteristics of one individual are determined by one's genes; and these can vary greatly among the billions of human beings who are conceived, gestate, and are born. Only in those rare instances when twins develop from the same fertilized egg can there be identical genotypes (the dissimilar twins coming from two eggs fertilized at the same time). Yet, even with identical twins, individuality is given to them by environmental factors in their nurture and personal development.

The emphasis upon the importance of genetic and personal individuality carries implications of a moral, social, and political character. It has long been accepted that in certain human activities and political systems the individuality of a man or woman is of no real concern. In past times, it did not matter who the men were who made up a crew of galley slaves, an army of foot soldiers, or a gang of manual laborers. If one died while at work or at war, he could be quickly and completely replaced by another. Names and faces were of no interest to taskmasters except for the purpose of keeping control over the men. In the present century, in the era of the totalitarian state, we have seen the encouragement of the same anonymity, but with far greater numbers of individuals affected than of yore. The same tendencies toward facelessness and replaceability have prevailed in the sweatshops and assembly-line factories of industrialized societies. The cry of millions has been basically for recognition of distinct personhood and emancipation from the undifferentiated human mass.

Lest this individuality be overemphasized and given exclusive importance for the essence of human life—that is, a doctrine of self-sufficient individualism—let it be balanced by the emphasis upon the oneness and solidarity of humanity. The inextricable, mutual relation between each individual and the whole human race, the complementary value of the unit and the totality of humanity, have been declared by pagan philosophers and biblical theologians alike since ancient times. The point was neatly expressed nearly nineteen centuries ago by the great Rabbi Akiba ben Joseph in a definitive statement:

> Whoever sustains a single person . . . is as one who sustains the whole world, and whoever destroys a single person is as one who destroys the whole world; for every person bears the divine image, and every person was created unique and irreplaceable.[3]

It is, therefore, not merely a figure of speech to refer to "the life of a nation" or even, as in John 6:51, "the life of the world," when "nation" and "world" refer to the totality of the human beings constituting them. Human life is at the same time a unity of the entire human species and the concrete life of each individual.

4. *Human life is the integrated unity of two kinds of components: first, all parts, organs, and systems of the physical organism that function, as presently understood, according to chemical actions; and, second, those intangible elements that are designated soul, spirit, mind, self-consciousness, will, and emotion.*

This statement evidently applies to human beings who are generally healthy and beyond the stage of infancy, since certain of the physical and intangible components are only beginning to develop then.

Precision of vocabulary concerning the intangible components is as difficult to achieve in English as in ancient Hebrew and

Greek. This remains so, despite the rapid modern mushrooming of knowledge about human life functions. Psychology has risen from being a branch of speculative philosophy to a disciplined, experimental science. Psychiatry has also grown as a medical specialty, accompanied and dependent on advances in the neurosciences. The new frontier of research is the brain itself, called by some scientists the most complex and enigmatic of all structures known in the universe thus far. Still, for lack of clearer understanding of those invisible sources of thinking, imagining, feeling, and behaving, we find that conventional words must serve to convey a sense of the diverse dimensions of life.

The philosophical theologian Paul Tillich referred to the given structures of life as "essentialist." He distinguished them from the "existentialist," which are the ambiguous conditions and experiences of living. As to the first, he included the essential components under the category, "the multidimensional unity of life."[4] As to the existential ambiguities, his thought might well have coincided with that which lay behind T. S. Eliot's poetic question: "Where is the Life we have lost in living?"[5] For Tillich, the goal of the harmonization of essential life and existential living can come at the end of the "quest for unambiguous or eternal life."[6] This clearly implies belief in the uniting and healing power of the divine life, which he describes as the Spiritual Presence. But one who admits to no traditional theistic faith or religious concern can employ this notion of the unity of essential and existential as the indicator of good health. The ancients spoke in simplest terms of "a healthy mind in a healthy body." Today, people who have acquired a knowledge of life's processes and of therapeutic measures which is vastly superior to that of the ancients can still advocate the view of wholistic health. Some presently prevailing concepts of health and healing are consonant with the insight concerning the multidimensional unity of life. "Whole person medicine" is based on this view of life, in contrast to that of a fragmented life, wherein physical, spiritual, and mental dimensions are seen separately.

5. Human life is characterized by potentiality; it is human being in process of human becoming.

The vexed yet decisive question that exacerbates the ongoing debate over the morality and legality of abortion is this: Is the embryo or fetus a human life? The answer given frequently and with much confidence is: It is *potential* life. The insufficiency and fallacy of this answer ought to be evident when analyzed carefully. A human embryo, or later a fetus, can be called potential life only if there is no life present already. But as we have seen in thesis 2 above, life has no starting point; it has only a mode of transmission from parent to offspring, and that is fertilization. The direction of the potential in the human zygote, early embryo, or fetus is not toward life; it is toward birth into personal existence in the world. The accurate way to state the matter is: *Not potential life, but life with potential.*

Toward what end is life's potential directed after birth? Obviously, as with all organic life, the potency of growth and development leads toward the maximum physical size and vigor which the species allows. Then its potential changes to the direction away from maximum strength toward senescence and eventual death. Thus it is with plants and organisms, including human beings, as the physical potentiality rises and declines in the individual's cycle of living.

The potentiality that characterizes human life clearly transcends the cycle of strength of cells, organs, and vital systems. This is because there can never be a consideration and definition of what life *is* without a linkage, however slight, to the *meaning* and *value* of life. The inherent ambiguity of the very word "human" shows the inevitability of this complexity. "Human" is both a definitive adjective for the species as well as a qualitative term designating the intellectual and moral norm and ideal of personal life. Potentiality means that, in this latter sense, human *being* and being *human* are always human *becoming* and becoming *human*. No one's life is ever fixed and final in form and status. It is always potential for becoming more human than it has been. The "is" of life is really a "to be" or a "to become," until death checks and ends the process of life. Yet, even that event of termination is not final, if the expectations for resurrection, based upon faith, prove to be valid.

WHAT IS THE *MEANING* OF LIFE?

1. *Humanness is the distinctive quality implied by the symbol of "the image of God," the image in which everyone is created and which is the presupposition of life's meaning; everyone's unique identity is the creation and endowment of God.*

What has been defined as life's being and becoming has already spoken to the question of meaning, but this can be specified and elaborated further.

The word "human" has both biological/physical and qualitative/ethical meaning. Even the most deliberate and consistent materialist can hardly avoid using it in both senses. As a taxonomical designation it is comparable to the adjectives "canine," "feline," "aquiline," and "ursine." They all apply to certain species. So does "human."

There is, however, a universal recognition of an ascending scale of meaning in the use of the word "human" as a qualitative and ethical indicator. It is thus qualified or modified by prefixes and adverbs. These convey our collective judgments of either condemnation or praise upon differing kinds of life and living by individuals. To be judged "inhuman" means that a person's attitude and actions are such as to violate and contradict the minimal, essential, moral character of humanity. "Subhuman" can be a shade less pejorative in the moral sense; or, it can denote other animals that are literally nonhuman but nevertheless approximate human intelligence and behavior. To be called "truly" or "authentically human" is to merit acknowledgment as one whose life and living are normative and exemplary with respect to virtuous and courageous conduct. Even this level of humanness can be exceeded by the few on whom the name "superhuman" is conferred. Thus cannibals, sadistic torturers, and mass murderers are called inhuman; child abusers, rapists, hit-and-run drivers, and warmongers are called subhuman; those who manifest high respect for all persons and act accordingly, while also developing their potential talents for aesthetic and intellectual enjoyment are said to be truly human, and self-sacrificing saints and the geniuses in generally approved fields of learning, the arts, and sciences are called superhuman. While it is evident that all of these are human in the meaning of species and physical form, the judgments we make about the humanness of people are relatively indifferent to the physical strength of their bodies. However, great feats of athletic prowess of physical agility and endurance can warrant the colloquial name superhuman.

The moral criteria for determining the meaning of human life within the spectrum from subhuman to superhuman are conditioned, to be sure, by cultural traditions which have been shaped in part by religious beliefs and teachings. The Christian influence upon the concept of humanness has been determined by the symbol of the "image of God," to which we referred in the next-to-last section of chapter 3. There is a cluster of interpretations of the meaning of this image, since Genesis does not provide one categorical interpretation, even while giving prominence to the image in the story of creation. But one aspect is clear and indisputable: it refers to the personal relationship that a man or woman may have with the Creator. The image of God is that quality in human life that makes possible this relationship. This implies, further, the inherent capacity for fellowship on the human plane, and notably that connection between man and woman, as Karl Barth has forcefully demonstrated.[7]

If humanness is thus equated with the created image of God in humanity generally and also in each individual, then the presupposition of life's meaning is that each one's unique identity is the creation and endowment of God. In order to have a personal relation with God and with one another, each of us needs to be a particular, unique person. Although we take this for granted, the explanation of individuality in all its dimensions of personality is not self-evident. Indeed, there is a deep mystery in each person. Thanks to the sciences of genetics and embryology, we now can understand the reasons for our physical characteristics, which set each of us apart from every other who ever existed. And further studies by endocrinologists, neurologists, and psychologists are revealing data that account for many aspects of the development of personality. However, the mystery of a person's capacity for relating to others eludes analysis. The "others" may be theoretically any other member of the human race, whether male or female, child or adult, of the same or of a different race, language, nationality, or culture, and whether the relationship be hostile, indifferent, civil, friendly, loving, or intimate. To be human is to have this capacity for relationship, except when disease or preventing circumstances interfere.

The fact of human relationship is so well known that the mystery of its possibility may not be problematical to most people. It is different with relationship to God. For many people, that is not only problematical; it is incredible. If God is infinite, how can finite people, limited by space and time, have personal communion with him? Or, to turn the question around, how is it conceivable that God can really know each human being and communicate over the barrier of finitude with every one of the four billion persons now living, as they are entering and leaving this terrestrial environment every second of time? Both questions stretch the mind's capacity for imagination and belief. They seem to demand that "sacrifice of the intellect" which is so repugnant to reasoning persons, who use the phrase as a slur against revealed religion. Biblical testimonies to the omniscience and omnipotence of God are impressive, but they only invite unquestioning faith. Does God really mark the fall of every sparrow? That was a hyperbolic statement by Jesus, no doubt. But does God really know the inner, secret thoughts of each person? If Christianity is justified in its claims about divine-human relationship and personal communion, it cannot tolerate a doctrine of God that implies any limitation upon God's power other than that which He creates and accepts. As for our believing what we cannot see, grasp, or understand, there are analogies in the mathematics of modern science that challenge our minds to cope with virtually infinite concepts. For astrophysics and microbiology there have been invented new units of measurement needed to count inconceivable distances and times. One angstrom is one ten-millionth of a millimeter. A billionth of a second can be measured as well as a billion light-years, which translate to 5^{21} miles. It is probably only a rhetorical question to ask whether the God who creates the universe can know individually some billions of human beings, who themselves are able to measure time and distance of inconceivable brevity, duration, and extension.

When Christians make statements about the meaning of life

being determined by creation in the image of such a God, they are affirming not only the divinity of infinite knowledge and power, but also the God whose goodness is stamped upon human beings as the definition of the humanness of their lives.

2. *This humanness includes the capacity for self-transcendence, which occurs in two dimensions:*

First, the ego, personally conscious and bearing a name, can reflect upon itself as a whole and upon the parts of the body or the ego itself, making judgments and decisions and projecting mental abstractions about itself.

If the capacity for personal relationship is indispensable for experiencing meaning in life, it includes not only two, but three, connections: between oneself and God; between oneself and other persons; and within oneself as both knower and known. Socrates' famous counsel, "Know thyself," and old Polonius's paternal advice to his son Laertes, "This above all, to thine own self be true," are the classic statements of the mystery of self-transcendence. But others abound in folklore and literature.

Reviewing the evidences of the evolution of the human species as revealed in the changing skeletal and cranial structures found in fossil remains, the Jesuit paleontologist Pierre Teilhard de Chardin proposed the thesis that true humanity began ages ago when this evolving hominid not only knew something, but knew that he knew it.[8] As to the time and circumstance of that momentous development, we can only imagine and speculate. It is manifestly impossible to discern vestiges of self-awareness in fossilized bones. Nevertheless, the compelling factor in Teilhard's thesis is the origin of the human self-consciousness. There is no real meaning to life where this is absent altogether, though consciousness may belong only to the potentiality of an unborn or newborn child, and self-awareness may be present at a minimal level in comatose adults.

The simple fact that a person can raise the question of what his or her life is, and of what meaning it has, is already part of the answer. To know that I know involves my knowing that I question; and my questioning implies knowledge of why I question and also of whether I hope for, or despair of, an answer. The convolutions and involutions of this line of such introspection can be explored further, virtually indefinitely, as one allows the imagination to run free. This process of wondering is a private experience of one's self-examining the self or conscious ego. It may, as we know, become an occasion for the self to pass judgments upon the self: self-criticism, self-hatred, self-satisfaction, self-congratulation, self-love, and self-preoccupation. There are many hyphenated affections. Without expressing any moral evaluation of this self-concern, at this point we only note and ponder its significance for the being and meaning of life.

Self-consciousness is inseparable from a name. The thought "I am" implies my name. My name is my identity. (In the new era of computerization we have not yet identified ourselves with our code numbers!) Not to have a name means that the answer to the deep question "Who am I?" is in effect "Nobody." Human life demands that everyone should be given a name. To be nameless is a condition that cannot last long in the company of another or others. Even a pseudonym is inevitable.

There is a numinous quality about a name. To invoke the name of a monarch, a pagan deity, Mohammed the Prophet, Jesus, or God in an oath or promise has meant to place complete trust in the invisible presence of the bearer of the name. For Judaism, the name of God is too holy even to be pronounced, so the Tetragrammaton YHVH is used as substitute and pronounced *Elohim* or *Adonai*. The conferring of a name on a baby is so essential that it early became identified in Christian practice with the rite of baptism; so the act of naming, "christening," often overshadowed the religious significance of the sacrament. In some Christian traditions of Eastern Orthodoxy, the "name day" is a more important celebration than the birthday.

Second, the exercising of physical and mental functions by each person involves an accumulation of significant experiences and creative acts that cannot be matched exactly by anyone else.

To the self-conscious and self-reflecting human life with the identity of a name is added the important factor of remembered experience. The significance of an individual's life is not merely enhanced by the power of memory; it is inescapably dependent upon the capability of storing the memories and accumulating experiences over stretches of many years. The brain is able to retain details and impressions of experiences even seven or eight decades after their occurrence, and to allow recall either deliberately or spontaneously. Just how the brain does this has not been explained. Neither is it known why an octogenarian may forget where he placed his glasses five minutes earlier but remember a place he visited only once when he was a boy. Often, instead of marveling at the phenomenon of this mystery we prefer to stand apart from ourselves and deplore the fallibility of "my poor memory." It should rather be the cause for amazement and gratification that anything at all of the past can be remembered with sufficient clarity to makes its instant recall useful for our present need. On the other hand, as often remarked, it would be a colossal overburden of the mind if we had the mental power of total recall of every previous experience. Therefore, computers with memory banks have been invented to extend the range of available data far beyond the normal capacity of one's brain and with a much faster rate of recalling. This is but one of the ways by which technology enlarges and enhances human life by extending the power of human faculties beyond their natural limits.

Whether able to remember too little or too much, each one's life can be described, from one perspective, as the accumulation of private experiences as well as of those shared by a few others or by many others. "In contrast to all other beings," wrote Tillich, "man does not have only environment; he has world, the structured unity of all possible content."[9] Each person's world, or personal cosmos, is unique in some respects. It is something "they can't take away from me," as people often say under duress, threat, or oppression. I *am* what I have done and experienced. My being and doing are inseparable.

3. *One's life can be fulfilled to any significant degree only when lived in relation to other persons in some form of mutually responsible community.*

Life's meaning cannot be expressed in the exclusive privacy of the individual's world, however precious the uniqueness of that person's life may be. It is virtually axiomatic for biblical anthropology as well as for other religious and secular views that human life is constitutionally, not incidentally, communal. A Christian interpretation of human community derives this universal reality from the Divine Being as such. The nature of the Triune God is love; and love is expressed initially and paradigmatically in the mutuality of the Father, and Son, and the Holy Spirit. Human affection within personal relations is thus the created image of the divine love. This is true whether that affection is between two persons, between man and woman, within a family, among those who are knit together in the oneness of Christ's church, or among persons in the numerous social groupings and relationships which make up society generally. Such relationships may not be felt as personal affection or intentional love, or of conscious participation in the divine gift of love. They may be maintained only for purposes of survival in social solidarity or in unreflective conformity to inherited cultural patterns of living. Nevertheless, these relationships may represent that essential bond of mutual dependency that characterizes all human life, not only the life which is defined in religious terms of community.

4. *Each person's creation by God is complemented by the "calling" of God to a life of responsibility and hope for the realization of one's potentiality.*

Colloquial expressions may be cited again to illustrate a profound insight about life and living. "You have missed your calling," is said to someone who unexpectedly shows a talent or skill of which others, and perhaps even the person addressed, had been unaware. There is some particular ability that the person has neither suspected nor suppressed; and eventually when it is released and cultivated, it becomes the primary motif of meaning for that person's whole life. "Calling" is thus equated with a certain aptitude, which might actually be traced to genetic inheritance or else referred to, without explanation, as a "gift." The gift presupposes a giver, who in Christian faith is God. Both terms, "calling" and "gift," entered our language from their original use in the New Testament. In vernacular usage they have been denuded of their theological vesture and come to mean only one's special ability and work or job. The connotation of a "vocational course" at school sums up the reduced sense of the originally abundant meaning of "calling" for one's life.

Work, occupation, creative and gainful activity are certainly essential for life and living. As such, they belong to one's calling from God, but they are only one aspect of the response to it. The apostle Paul wrote, "let every one lead the life which the Lord has assigned to him, and in which God has called him" (1 Cor. 7:17). What he meant was evidently not just a job or mode of employment. Nor did he refer to working people only, since the address of the statement is to "every one." In another context and letter the people are summoned "to lead a life worthy of the calling to which you have been called" (Eph. 4:1). The sense is clear. God's calling is not a general moral appeal to all human beings, but a particular call to each one in his or her time, place, status, and circumstance. God calls each by name. This means that the gifts and talents that each has received from God by creation and by spiritual grace are to be effectively and responsibly employed in the realizing of a life approved of God. But this requires more than a strong determination, ambition, or moral will. It requires such commitment and openness to God's presence in Jesus Christ that the person can receive, without the common hindrances of anxiety or pride, what in chapter 4 we called the divine gift of abundant, fulfilled life.

5. *Life's quality is discerned in the three dimensions suggested, though not defined, by the three Greek words for "life" used in the New Testament:* Bios *meaning subsistence or bare survival;* Psuchē *meaning enjoyment of the experiences of individual, familial, and social living with more than the minimal degree of health, activity, and expectation; and* Zōē *meaning life being fulfilled already through participation in the eternal quality of living as, according to Christian faith, it is willed and offered by God in Jesus Christ.*

All human beings living in these dimensions owe life to creation by God; all are intrinsically human and precious in God's sight; and all are subject to conditions of growth, maturation, health, culture, social circumstance, and self-awareness. All have "quality," but that word merits critical analysis before it can be illuminating.

In English society of past centuries, "a person of quality" was a man or woman who was highborn, cultured, rich, and of lofty social status. That aristocratic definition has been fully democratized in our time. It has been displaced by the phrase "quality of life'' which has become part of our contemporary jargon. Jargon is an epidemic disease of language. It disrupts the health of reasonable speech and, like cholera, its spread is most difficult to arrest. Jargon words do not define their referent but conceal its meaning. While "quality of life" seems to say something about what makes human life and living good, it actually conceals that meaning by its unchallenged assumption that all people know what it means. In fact, they do not. There is very little agreement on what ingredients constitute a life of quality. People hold diametrically opposed notions. Thus, there can be no agreement on the amount, or the degree of attainment or of excellence of these undefined ingredients needed for a satisfying quality.

"Quality of life" not only begs the question of life's meaning; it is a slippery phrase. Primarily and simply, "quality" refers to an attribute or characteristic of some thing or some one. It is used neutrally until it is modified by an adjective that expresses an evaluative judgment. Is this person's quality of life good or bad, high or low, tolerable or hopeless? Used by itself, "quality" tells us nothing. It must be filled with ideas of evaluation.

"Quality of life" is not only a slippery concept; it is also ambiguous. In present usage it applies either to the economic, social, and political conditions of a society or nation, or to individual human beings. In discussions and debates over issues of bioethics, however, the two uses often tend to be confused.

The first use of quality of life is aptly illustrated, for example, in a publication of the United Nations Educational, Social and Cultural Organization:

> Comfortable housing (from 30 to 100 m² per family, according to the wealth of the country, with light or ventilation, running water, plumbing, heating if necessary and even—an unheard-of luxury for half the people of the world—electricity); communications, proximity of shopping centres and public amenities of various kinds (educational, public health, sports, cultural, religious, administrative).[10]

That this environmental understanding of quality of life is shared by Americans was shown by a Louis Harris opinion poll. The tabulations revealed that 44 percent of the respondents judged the quality of life to be worsening; and the five main factors which

138

they considered of critical importance were: air and water pollution, public education, energy supplies, privacy, and safety in working conditions.[11] Thus, quality is seen by many, perhaps most, people to apply to our environment and modes of living. But the quality of *life* or of personal *human being* as such receives relatively little attention. Ecological, economic, and educational concerns which dominate this interpretation are manifestly of much importance. But are they *life*?

As applied to individual human beings, "quality of life" has a philosophical, psychological, and theological sense. It pertains to the satisfaction, happiness, meaning, or purpose that one finds, or might possibly find, in living. The factors that are evaluated to make such determination are: the individual's genetic, physical endowment; family and home environment; the social milieu in which the person lives or might live; ecological environment; and the intellectual, aesthetic, and spiritual development of the person.[12]

Only in this latter sense is it reasonable to contrast "quality of life" with the "value" or "sanctity" of life. Then it is often proposed that a strongly negative judgment about the quality of one's genotype, physiology, mental capacity, family relations, social milieu, or integrity as a self-conscious person should suffice to deny continued life to an unborn or newly born child, a drastically deformed or incapacitated person, or one who is both aged and infirm. Then the perceived or putative prospects for a good, happy, and useful life with significant meaning are weighed against the belief, which prevails in most cultures and societies, that each human life in whatever condition has intrinsic, inalienable worth.

Neither of the two uses of "quality of life" succeeds in revealing what it is that makes human life genuinely human. They both deal almost entirely with the external conditions of environment and of physical health, to the neglect of the inner *qualities* which are most determinative in shaping *who* a person is or can become.

Until there can be developed a generally acceptable conception or definition of quality of life that takes into account *all* of life's dimensions, it remains an utterly relative and confusing norm.

Indeed, at present it is no norm at all. Good health, unimpaired physical capability and appearance, the love and approval of parents, a congenial home, financial security—all these are factors contributing to a truly human and authentic life. However much they are appreciated, though, they are not self-evidently necessary to a life of true quality. Many people having such benefits have come to ruin and tragic death. And among the greatest leaders of religion, art, music, science, and politics in all human history have lived persons who were friendless, impoverished, chronically ill, blind, deaf, imprisoned, persecuted, and even doomed by congenital diseases to fits of madness and early death.

The quality of life consists primarily in dimensions of the mind, the spirit, the senses, and affections, rather than in convenience and comfort. We can distinguish three levels of human life, which must be designated in English by the same word "life": sheer physical existence, which is shared with the animals and except for the disposition of the mind may seem to be no more than subsistence and survival; the daily experience of work, moral decision, family and social obligations, diversion, love, and joy; and the realizing of potentialities for human service and affection, constructive achievement, moral integrity, aesthetic creativity, spiritual experience, and harmonious communion with God.

As *bios, psuchē*, and *zōē* were presented in chapter 4, they are not strictly religious terms, reserved for Bible readers and believers; they are not limited in their applicability to the elect. Rather, they indicate the dimensions of life's meaning as influenced, to be sure, by environment and situation, but also as informed by the working of God's Spirit upon the individual and by the receptivity of his or her whole person to the divine offer of *zōē*. Just as the English language can designate life as biological and psychic, the idea derived from the New Testament of life full of meaning can be called "zoetic."

WHAT IS THE *VALUE* OF LIFE?

1. *The unique integrity of each human being, as created and loved by God and capable in maturity of enjoying community with*

others and communion with God, corresponds to the essential sanctity of life.

In current disputes over capital punishment, abortion, infanticide, and assisting in the hastening of death, it is remarkable how frequently people on opposing sides appeal to the same standards of the intrinsic value, dignity, sacredness, or sanctity of human life. No sensible, moral person wants to be regarded as antilife or lenient toward killing. Yet, it seems to be just as possible to argue for the death of a fetus, a "defective" newborn, a comatose patient, one with a terminal illness, or even a criminal by claiming respect for the sanctity of life as it is to defend life by the same claim. Sissela Bok muses on the evidence "that everyone, including those who authorize or perform the most brutal killings in war, can protest their belief in life's sacredness."[13] If all the disputants could agree on what is meant by value, dignity, sacredness, and sanctity, most such arguments could be settled forthwith. It is not these evaluative words as such that divide people, but the diverse senses in which they are used. And not only the definitions of the words, but the total concepts of life, both general and human, which are at variance, constitute the barriers to understanding and agreement.

Such terms as "value" and "dignity" of life do not necessarily depend upon religious beliefs. They are used responsibly by persons who either candidly profess agnosticism about any divinity or else firmly support atheism. They are satisfied with a humanistic philosophy, whereby certain goods and values are perceived to inhere in the basic facts of life, which are just physical existence and mental awareness and cognition. Their moral views about life and death are shaped by such perceptions, independent of any appeal to divinely revealed truth. Indeed, it is not uncommon for nonreligious humanists to assert that *their* convictions about human value and dignity are superior to those of such Christians or other believers whom they regard as hypocrites. Moreover, it would be, it is, inexcusably insensitive and arrogant for professing Christians to disparage the humane and humanistic values of nonbelievers.

There is a difference, nevertheless, that needs to be examined.

For example, Christians may gladly admit that nonbelievers hold valid and even lofty ideals of life's dignity and value. After all, the moral heritage of our collective history does not come to us as nihilism or despair about life's goodness and meaning. That Christians might justly yet modestly assume that their concept of the sanctity of life transcends that of dignity, worth, or value need not, to be sure, provoke rebuttal. Is not "sanctity" by definition a religious term? In the most prominent British and American dictionaries it is defined entirely in a religious sense, admitting no secular meaning. Does it not necessarily relate human life, or even all organic life, to the divine source?

Contrary to some expectations, secular writers can seriously extol the *sanctity* of life without acknowledging any reference to divinity. In a rather daring essay Edward Shils, a noted sociologist, declares himself to be fully skeptical of Christian or other religious belief; yet he stoutly affirms the sacredness, or sanctity, of life. This estimation arose in humanity's long historical experience from what he calls a deep "proto-religious, 'natural metaphysics.'" As for the Christian doctrine of sanctity, it "was enabled to maintain its long prosperity and to become effective because it was able to conform for so many centuries" to that natural insight.[14] For Shils, the words "sacred" and "sanctity" by themselves carry the full weight of awe and reverence toward human life without any theological props at all. It is an evident axiom for him that "if life is not viewed and experienced as sacred, then nothing else would be sacred."[15] Yet, this is not an absolute value for Shils:

> Some lives are regarded as more sacred than others. . . . There is a gradation of "sanctity" moving from the individual outward—first through his kinship and affectional attachments, then local, national, class, ethnic group and culture, becoming more attenuated and patchier as it reaches into other countries, continents and races.[16]

Two philosophers who have analyzed the nuances and implications of the nonreligious idea of sanctity of life are Daniel Callahan[17] and William K. Frankena.[18] Callahan agrees with Shils up to a point. He welcomes the principle of sanctity of life as one on which an approach to moral consensus can be based.[19] And he sees how the intensity of moral concern for respecting and protecting life varies from the concern for an individual's personal integrity to that for family lineage and the whole human race or species. However, Callahan finds Shils's claim to the self-evident sacredness of life to be question begging. To say that human life is sacred because it is sacred is logically, as Frankena also judges, a tautology.[20]

Is it so, that the prevalence of the idea of sanctity is due, after all, to the influence of the biblically informed faith of Judaism and Christianity upon the moral attitudes of European and American culture? If so, it is no longer the case that the dominance of the widely held religious faith determines respect for life, because Christianity has been in a century-long recession. But the roots still live, according to popular theory, and the vestiges of their moral fruit continue to be borne. Or else, in the more extreme "cut flower" theory of post-Christian culture, even the roots of religion are detached and withering. Would the disappearance of all faith lead to the total loss of belief in life's sanctity? In the theological sense of that word, yes; in its secular use, not necessarily. Frankena not only recognizes how secularists espouse the concept; he proposes a partially nonreligious origin of it. He suggests that it was in three great movements of thought and mood that the devotion to life as such found modern impetus: this-worldly vitality of the Renaissance; the aesthetic Romanticism and philosophical idealism in the early nineteenth century; and the spirit of evolutionism after Darwin.[21] From these three developed a kind of "eulogistic use of the word *life*" and ascription of "a kind of sanctity to life, human or nonhuman." Frankena judges this kind of thought, which arises from the vigor of observed organisms and the sheer liveliness of human life, to be uncompelling as a reason for holding to the moral sanctity of life. It is as unpersuasive as the contrasting teaching of the Christian church, that all human life comes from God and belongs finally to Him. Apart from these alternatives, Frankena still finds cause to hold human life, including fetal life, in high but qualified respect. The qualification is the possibility to attain "something more" than mere bodily life. The "something more" is conceivable only in the experiences that add up to a general sense of the "quality of life."[22]

Some idea of value or sanctity of life is held by people of sensitivity and sympathy, by those who have a sense of wonder at life's complexity and of justice for all individuals. Whatever their religious faith or ecclesial persuasion, they respect human life. Why?

Philosophers have offered their theories without reference to God. In popular Christian, Jewish (and Muslim) discourse, belief is expressed very simply by two dogmatic clichés: Life is a gift of God, and we are made in God's image. For religious believers, these affirmations are not susceptible of scientific or philosophical demonstration on the grounds of observation, experience, and reflection. They are statements of faith alone, and that in two ways: first, they presuppose the reality of God; second, they assume the special creative acts of God which bring each human being into existence. If, as often happens, the moral attitudes toward human life which are held by both believer and nonbeliever should coincide—as, for example, in condemning suicide or opposing capital punishment—what difference does it make to call life the gift of God and profess the divine image? Practically, in many cases, none. Believers and nonbelievers can engage side by side in the political effort to oppose laws permitting the killing of criminals. Yet, as Callahan rightly sees, there are "two fundamentally different world-views" represented.[23] The contrast is between human wisdom and divine will communicated by revelation. What does that contrast mean? It does not imply that when people encounter certain medical, social, or bioethical problems they will have available to them some ready-made guidelines or even specific answers, one set coming by revelation from God, the other from prudential reasoning. We know how believing communities, Christian as well as Jewish, are divided among themselves. In disagreement with the teachings or policies of their own religious bodies, many members prefer to join secular humanists on the critical issues of abortion and the prolonging of the process of dying. The level of approximation to consensus within a Christian church or a council of synagogues depends upon several variables: numerical size of membership, cultural diversities, concepts of official doctrinal authority as distinct from private judgment, and the power of whatever controlling commitments distinguish the body from others. Eastern Orthodox, Roman Catholics, Lutherans, Protestant "peace churches," and Orthodox Jews tend toward homogeneity. Other Protestants and more liberal Jews show much diversity.

Does the lack of religious consensus indicate, then, the irrelevance of common faith in God as the righteous Deity who reveals truth about life? Not at all. The relevance of faith for ethics is found in the common acknowledgment of God's authority as apprehended in the Bible and the church traditions. Disagreeing Christians of whatever denomination or confession know themselves to be subject to the divine will. Their contrary insights and convictions always stand under the possibility of being corrected and reformed by the word of God. Even widely held notions such as the justification of slavery or the attributing of God's special favor to certain armies in warfare have been cogently exposed as a distortion of the Christian faith in God's purposes. So it may be with the present attitudes held by many Christians, attitudes that disregard the sanctity of human life or else subordinate it to the psychological, economic, or political factors which may be involved in making judgments about the so-called quality of life.

2. *Each one holds a lease on life as a loan from God, and thus assumes as a trust the living of that life throughout its earthly, temporal existence.*

In setting forth and defending the high respect for human life, some Christian zealots are inclined to overstate the case. They appear to advocate the idea that life's sanctity is wholly intrinsic to the living organism as such, whatever the stage of the life span or the physical conditions. Thus, the unqualified defense and unconditional preservation of every individual of the human species is construed to be faithful obedience to God's primary and exclusive command. This belief in a divinely ordained human vitalism is really a caricature of Christian teaching. It expresses Albert Schweitzer's unreserved "reverence" for all life rather than Christianity's "sanctity" of human life, however similar those words may seem.

For Christian faith, the idea is fundamental that God creates each one, imprints the divine image which is the essence of humanness, and bestows life in its full dimensions as a gift. This gift takes priority over all other divine gifts, for it is the necessary presupposition of one's very existence. The gift of life is never without "strings," however. It is the free gift of God, since we cannot determine by ourselves the beginning of our individual existence and identity. Yet the gift is always accompanied by obligations of responsibility to God for maintaining one's life and using all its powers in ways congruent with God's known will. To make this distinction clear, Karl Barth in his extended discussion of "Respect for Life" insists repeatedly that life is not an outright gift from God, but rather a *loan*.[24] The distinction between gift and loan is important. It can be understood readily when we think of familiar analogies to giving and lending, receiving and borrowing. The gift once given is beyond the reach and control of the giver. But the loan, once extended, remains the property of the lender until a settlement is made. Hence, the sacred or holy aspect of human life which merits the name sanctity inheres neither in our simply having it nor even in its being created by God. If everything created by God is called sacred, there remains no particular sanctity of human life. Barth's emphasis upon life as God's loan conveys the extremely important belief that God still owns each life. It is the ownership that conveys sanctity to it.

Some Protestant theologians conclude from the insight about life as a loan that the value, dignity, or sanctity is not located or contained in human life intrinsically. It is extrinsic; it is "alien." Life belongs only to God. This is how the apostle Paul perceived both the moral quality of life—righteousness—and the existence of one's life. Any righteousness that I may manifest is not "a righteousness of my own," he wrote, but is "the righteousness of God which depends on faith" (Phil. 3:9). In the same vein, Paul counseled the new Christians at Corinth: "you are not your own" (1 Cor. 6:19). Martin Luther called this "alien righteousness," and some think that it can correspond with the "alien sanctity" of life. At least, there is an obvious parallelism between the two notions. As Luther restated Paul's insight on justification by grace and faith alone, the fulcrum of the Reformation, his teaching was vigorously opposed by Roman Catholics. Justification—to be made right with God—is an *imputed* righteousness, Luther asserted, because we can claim no true righteousness of our own, but only Christ's. The Catholic Council of Trent retorted, righteousness is *imparted* by the infused grace of God. This latter interpretation is congenial to the Catholic theory of natural law, with which Protestants have long felt uneasy, lest the creation and the human creature be unduly exalted before the Creator.

To hold that the sanctity of life is imparted to each human being is more in line with natural law theory than that sanctity is imputed by the continuing relation through the Redeemer Jesus Christ with the Creator God. Thus, the Catholic moralist Charles E. Curran finds fault with the idea of "alien dignity" because he does not want the Christian way of valuing life to be so exclusive as to minimize other human ways, ways based not on a theological affirmation but on "criteria inherent in individual human life."[25] His concern is a just one.

Is it not a misconception of the intention of this Protestant theology of life, though, to assume that life's sanctity, whether imputed or imparted, alien or proper, applies only to persons who embrace faith in Jesus Christ? Barth, to be sure, never hesitates to interpret the whole of human life in relation to God's work and presence through Jesus Christ. From the perspective of Christian faith, everyone is included in Jesus Christ, whether or not one knows this; for the Christian affirmation is not about a certain man and religious prophet named Jesus, but about the Triune God:

> What matters is not something but someone, the real man before God and among his fellows, his individual psychophysical existence, his movement in time, his freedom, his orientation on God and solidarity with others. What matters is that everyone should treat his existence and that of every other human being with respect. For it belongs to God. It is His loan and blessing. And it may be seen to be this in the fact that God Himself has so unequivocally and completely acknowledged it in Jesus Christ.[26]

3. *Health is valued as the requisite strength for the proper func-*

tioning of the body and mind, enabling the person to realize and experience a genuinely human existence; defects in health are not always detrimental, but in some cases can serve the same good end.

"Health" is like "life" in the sense that all people think they know what it is but they cannot agree on its definition. To say that health is indispensable to life is utterly obvious; but this does not mean life's value, or even sanctity, is proportionate to the degree of good health attained on some scale leading to an ideal of perfection. The statistical conception of health, as measured by indicators of one's nearness to some normative ideal, is presently a popular conception. Specialists set the standards of body weight in relation to height; blood pressure; quantities of sugars, salts, acids, cholesterol, iodine, calcium, iron, and other vital chemicals; accuracy of vision and hearing; and so on down the chart of health. When, after a complete examination, one receives "a clean bill of health," it is widely understood that the ideal is not far away.

To the norms of metabolism, cardiovascular and respiratory regularity, and other vital functions health enthusiasts add, in the second place, the aesthetic appearances. Textured skin over supple muscles, glossy hair, straight teeth, trim waistline, full breasts, firm cheeks, well-shaped ears and nose are the prominent factors in appraising aesthetic health. Ostensibly related to sexual attractiveness and powers, these are made as important for health as physical functioning, to the profit of cosmeticians and plastic surgeons, and to the sad despair of the incorrigibly disabled, obese, bald, flat-chested, and the undoubtedly unattractive.

Function and appearance, however, are not enough to satisfy a third conception of health, namely mental health. Freedom from anxiety and depression, or from such gross psychopathological afflictions as paranoia and schizophrenia, is thus added to the requisites of good health status.

Since psychic condition affects behavior, and behavior raises the question of acting according to a society's moral standards, the definition of health takes on a fourth dimension in addition to function, appearance, and mental state. But how is an individual's moral disposition—to conform or to defy the standards—determined? By genetic inheritance? by nurturing environment in family, school, circles of playmates and friends? by economic status? by mass media—printed, cinematic, electronic? by the political character of a society or nation? by religion? None of these is self-evidently the cause of specified moral behavior; yet each plays some role in determining a person's moral health.

The concept of health for many people has by now come to mean almost everything one experiences in life's elusive struggle and quest to attain the ideal body, mind, and situation of social well-being—in short, *happiness*.

The essentially hedonistic notion of health which motivates many people in the rich and technically developed countries, particularly in Europe and North America, is almost inevitably also narcissistic. One loves one's body, face, and feeling of vigor so long as these are in accord with the ideal norms; but self-love breeds anxiety and despair when infirmity, aging, or the dissolution resulting from failure of self-care discipline prevail.

There is well-attested evidence about the disposition of some men and women who have been free from serious illness or physical impairment; who are virtual paragons of attractive beauty; who have never even met a psychiatrist except at social occasions; who have neither a nagging bad conscience nor a police record; who have never known the economic shortages which prevent their having adequate food, higher education, comfortable housing, family support, travel, and cultural expression; who have always been citizens of a democratic nation. The evidence is just that they are *not* happy with such quality of life. Are they then not healthy?

According to a rather limited, old-fashioned idea, persons were considered to be healthy when their whole organism functioned well enough for them to live and keep occupied. The temporary alternative to good health was morbidity due to disease, infection, or accident; the enduring alternative was severe disability; the final alternative was mortality. Health was simply having the requisite strength to live. A more sophisticated statement of this essential idea of health is that of the sociologist Talcott Parsons, who used the biological thesis of Ernst Mayr:

> I should like to venture to put forward a tentative definition of health. It may . . . be conceived as the teleonomic capacity of an individual living system. The teleonomic capacity that we wish to call health is a capacity to maintain a favorable, self-regulated state, which is a prerequisite of the effective performance of an indefinitely wide range of functions both within the system and in relation to its environments.[27]

The polar opposite of that basic conception was defined in 1946 by the constitution of the World Health Organization. This definition has been frivolously lampooned, seriously criticized, and fulsomely praised. For many it remains a self-evident truth, like human equality, that "Health is a state of complete physical, mental and social well-being, and not merely the absence of disease or infirmity."[28] The critical word in this sentence is "complete." Who knows what complete social well-being is? Even the physical is hard to define. And the mental? Yet, the approval accorded this WHO conception was revealed by a most inclusive study conducted by the Christian Medical Commission of the World Council of Churches. Its summary report declared that the WHO definition "should be expanded to include the spiritual dimension," and even go beyond that. Thus it is proposed that health is "a dynamic state of well-being of the individual and of the society; of physical, mental, spiritual, economic, political and social well-being; of being in harmony with each other, with the material environment, and with God."[29] As these many ingredients of a full concept of health accumulate, it becomes clear that if health means everything good in life it really means nothing in particular.

Conversely, as the opposite of an all-inclusive definition, a fully comprehensive catalogue of threats to social well-being can become indistinguishable from all the negative influences upon the organism's physical functioning and the causes of death. Of the five main causes of death among young adults, for example, only one—cancer—is a disease subject to medical therapy. The other four are motor vehicle accidents, other kinds of accidents, homicides, and suicides. How can good or poor health be attributed to the victims of violence, whether of their own or another's making? Behind these causes of death are numerous other factors, often subsumed together under the jargon term "life style," which defy measurement. Alcoholism is clearly a disease, but the act of not fastening a seat belt in a car is not. Are both of these aids to death to be regarded as life style?

Other confusions attend the comprehensive definition of health and carry with them a note of irony. The nation's epidemiological monitoring is done by the Center for Disease Control. This constant survey includes the rate of abortions per hundred thousand pregnancies. Is an unwanted child, then, a product of disease, a disease called pregnancy? Another example is considered in macroeconomic terms: The second highest expenditure after the United States' military budget is the nation's bill for overall health care. The costs of "the medical-industrial complex" are so widely discussed and so far beyond a person's comprehension that they need no illustrating or emphasizing. But the irony lies in the realization, upon which many physicians are now acting, that the ultimate threat to health is precisely that to which much of the military budget is currently dedicated—nuclear weapons.

The comprehensive definition certainly implies a laudable intention: a fully human, happy existence for every person. However, as it becomes increasingly inclusive of all factors making for a good life, it becomes decreasingly useful as a measure of an individual's actual health condition and process of improvement. Furthermore, the preferability of a simple definition of strength for living is amplified when we consider how defects in health, at least in some cases, can also serve the purpose of promoting human existence. Such evidence must be weighed most carefully, lest the false impression be given that hardships, disabilities, and diseases are to be enjoyed. But enjoyment is not the only concern here. Meaning and value of life are frequently expressed dramatically through disability, difficult struggle, and even through suffering. People can achieve the enhanced life not only in spite of, but sometimes because of, the seeming counterweights of health.

4. *While no human life may be judged to be worthless, each*

being of inestimable value, the conditions of ambiguous existence and moral imperfection often require choices to be made between two or more lives, each choice having to be made seriously on the merits of the case.

How can a reasonable and defensible choice be made between two lives of the same infinite value? Ideally, we should not have to raise this question. In fact, it arises in countless instances. Not only in clinical medicine and in catastrophic emergencies must choices be made and a balance of life's value sought, but in the whole economic order and in courts of law and international relations. The entire texture of human social living is shot through with situations of hard choice or of actual dilemma. In terms of nutrition, health care, and opportunity just to live or to live well, the principle of each person's inestimable value is constantly strained. Life as such is not the absolute value above all others, but it comes close to being so. Yet, the almost absolute value of people's lives, determined by their sanctity, is in fact conditioned by many circumstances which elevate concerns for honor, justice, liberty, and faithfulness above those of elemental humaneness. In this world of ambiguous existence and moral imperfection it is clear that everyone cannot enjoy everything desired, even though one's essential life is valued beyond measurement. From this ineluctable contradiction come the numerous problems of ethics. They are only noted in general here, lest zeal for expanding the value and sanctity of all life and every life conceal the grim realities of our mortal existence.

5. *Life's great value is the possibility, in consequence of death and by God's grace and creating power, to be resurrected to new life.*

The yearning for unending life is nearly, but not quite, universal in human experience. Not everyone seeks immortality. Not everyone believes in its possibility; when life ends, it ends—abandon hope here! But where there is no hope there is no life. Theories of the dignity, value, and even (as we have seen) sanctity of life must then be bounded by the two horizons of birth and death.

Christianity is the religion of resurrection. It offers neither an empty agnosticism about life beyond this temporal existence nor a bland assurance of the inevitable immortality of the soul. Instead, it kindles the hope of *zōē aiōnios*, fulfilled eternal life, by the resurrection which it proclaims. Just as God creates each life within the finite frame of the created cosmos, so the same divine power works through Jesus Christ to create anew those who have died.

6

FROM GENESIS TO GENETICS:
A THEOLOGICAL-ETHICAL
EXERCISE

To persons who make hard decisions intuitively rather than deductively the statement is jokingly attributed: "Don't bother me with the facts." Even more than the facts such persons would disdain the counsels of theology and religious ethics. The truth is, however, that decisions in the fields of human experimentation, medical practice, and genetic manipulation cannot be made intuitively. A large amount of scientific data must be gathered for consideration before undertaking procedures or experiments which may put at risk either human well-being or human life. Yet, scientific knowledge and technical data alone do not suffice in taking the measure of matters of life and death in the clinic or the laboratory. It is the thesis of this book that a theory of human life, whether philosophical or theological or both, is indispensable to the reaching of valid decisions of a bioethical nature.

Persons who are exposed to the printed and electronic news media need no primary tutoring in the present and possible achievements of the newly developed recombinant-DNA technique, nor of its putative benefits and perils. Not only have some molecular biologists of the first magnitude become executives of corporate enterprises in the genetic field; they have been writing and speaking out as sagacious prophets of either promise or doom. Into the vortex of their vigorous and sometimes acrimonious debates have been drawn many "concerned citizens," legislators, venture capitalists, and the studious philosophers and theologians of ethics. Molecular biology is no longer a "pure" science, a disinterested pursuit of the "truth" of natural phenomena. This discipline, writes the concerned biochemist Liebe F. Cavalieri "was transformed, virtually overnight, into a force that not only can examine the living organism but now can manipulate the organism in ways never before possible at the will of the scientist."[1] And he adds the trenchant remark, "For many biological scientists, recombinant-DNA technology has brought the societal implications of biological research close to home for the first time."

The Supreme Court has decreed that so-called new life forms may come within the protection of the federal patent laws.[2] The legal green light was thus flashed to the spontaneously generated genetic industries, numbering now some one hundred fifty. What may their patenting of novel bacteria and organic cells eventually mean for the public?

Since the chemical ingredients of all DNA molecules are the same, varying only in numbers and arrangements, it is feasible to modify cells of numerous species, both plant and animal, by inserting selected genes into host cells and creating strange hybrids, or chimeras. However, does anyone know for sure whether there are natural "species barriers" which ought to be respected, lest evolutionary processes and ecological balances be disrupted? Even the genes of Homo sapiens can be blended with those of plants and animals. These laboratory procedures may affect only some cell samples in petri dishes. But may they not lead to modifications of germ cells in the organisms, including the human, which they reproduce irretrievably as altered species? This prospect may appeal in theory to the advocates of planned eugenics for the human race, but in reality may cause dysgenic results. Without controlled experimentation who can know? But how can testing be achieved with sufficient reassurance when the human generational cycle is about twenty years? Will testing on mice or monkeys suffice?

Or consider the use of gene splicing for therapeutic purposes in the realm of genetic medicine. No one but a misanthrope can in principle take a stand against therapeutic medicine. Employing genetic materials, experts in microsurgery, working on human beings at embryonic or fetal stages, can prevent some of the more than two thousand known genetic diseases. But what are the costs and risks involved?

Such questions, both hypothetical and already encountered, only illustrate why people are increasingly expressing moral and social concern. The risks go beyond and are more difficult to resolve than the much-discussed dangers of biohazards in and out of laboratories, risks which during the past decade have alerted the scientific community, legislators, and the public.

Can it be rightly said that these questions are all in some way religious questions? Yes. Are they to be resolved exclusively within the province of religious thought? Of course not. But, as will be demonstrated below, there is a deliberate, systematic way of theological reasoning that leads to some definite positions on the implications of genetic engineering in particular.

Faith in the "image of God" as the mold in which human beings are cast fundamentally determines the moral stance of both Jews and Christians. Depending upon one's understanding of the biblical and theological teaching, this phrase can be either a pious but mindless cliché or a profound affirmation packed with meaning. One common understanding of the image of God, as we have seen, is just that the human distinctiveness, derived from our creation in God's image, is our ability to reason and to choose between good and evil, to have knowledge about ourselves, to communicate with others, and to be aware of destiny. Closely related is the belief that the image of God is that quality of life that constitutes the human dignity which all scientists, regardless of belief, should respect. Catholic theology holds that this dignity bestowed by creation in God's image is a matter of natural law and thus the basis for ethical reasoning about human life. Knowledge of it is accessible to all persons through reason and is not derived from a particular divine revelation.

Other interpreters of the image would not so much disagree with these general premises as move beyond them to more specifically defined concepts and beliefs. The popular phrases discussed above—"reverence for life," "gift of life," "sanctity of life," "playing God," and even "image of God"—are only crude pointers toward the carefully nuanced theology that empowers and guides ethical reasoning. Religious thinkers, including diverse types of Jews and Christians, are realizing tardily but not too late that faith and theology have a definite pertinence to science in general and to genetic technology in particular.

Ethical evaluations are not deduced by logical process from given dogmatic propositions; neither do they arise from intuitive thought about the problems posed by scientific techniques. Rather, the ethical positions are worked out by persons of faith and knowledge who can subject theological concepts to the challenge of technology and, conversely, submit technology to critical judgment. Methodological help in the direction of such thinking was provided by the late Paul Tillich's idea of correlation between existential human problems and the insights of faith and theology. Correlation involves an interaction, a dialectical give and take, between the realms of religious thought and scientific technology. Each has an effect upon the other, and both are needed to formulate positions which will be equally congruent with religious faith and related to current practices in the fields of microbiology and applied genetics.

A distinction should be drawn here between faith and theology, although the two belong together. Faith is both an attitude and a body of concepts; it is a combination of biblical and traditional teachings which are personally accepted as true—teachings which because they are ultimately important for one's self-understanding and for directing one's life in human society warrant the person's wagering everything upon their veracity and upon the God to whom they point. Theology is the intellectual effort expended to clarify and interpret these beliefs in which people place their trust; it is expressed in as reasonable a way as possible and in terms appropriate to particular cultures.

Christian theology has no ready-made solutions to the problems being posed by the sudden advent of the science of genetic engineering. There has been insufficient time for theologians to understand and assess the issues. The untimely expression of categorical judgments must be regarded with caution, since few theologians and ethicists have a clear grasp of the microbiological data concerned, or of the human physiological information, or the social, economic, and legal factors which are germane to the whole complex of issues. Yet the challenge to theology is an urgently demanding one.

No single exposition can adequately represent all shades of Christian theology, which range over the entire spectrum from biblical dogmatism on one side to a reduced religious philosophy on the other. The pluralism and tolerance of much Christian thought are both its shame and its glory. There is no single authority for teaching, neither an ecclesiastical body nor the literal verses of the Bible. Yet much of traditional so-called mainline Protestantism shares a general common system of beliefs. Moreover, this kind of Protestantism keeps open to and appreciative of other Christian teachings, other religious teachings, and other congenial philosophical insights; and it is cognizant of the great importance of scientific research and technology for human knowledge and well-being.

THEOLOGICAL AFFIRMATIONS RELEVANT TO GENETIC ENGINEERING

Certain elements of Christian belief and theological understanding are clearly germane to the discussion of the implications of genetic engineering. These are not categorical propositions from which ethical conclusions are logically deduced. They are, rather, affirmations that influence the kind of reflective and unprecedented thinking that scientific achievement now requires. How they can be correlated to questions about genetics will be shown later.

Creation

The earth and all that it contains as well as the entire universe of which it and we are a part, exist only because of the exercise of divine power, will, and purpose. Neither blind chance nor inexorable necessity accounts for the world's origin or existence. The research, findings, and theories of scientists need to be treated with full seriousness; but they neither annul nor displace, nor vindicate the Christian belief in creation.

The special place of humanity within the universe is validated by the quality of freedom. This is the freedom of God to actualize the divine creative omnipotence, a creativity which within appropriate temporal and mortal limits has been conferred upon human beings as their freedom to act creatively.

Humanity

Human freedom, creative intelligence, intellectual self-transcendence, and love are ultimately inexplicable, however profoundly we may theorize about them. They are distinctive qualities of human beings. We can attest, describe, and appraise them; but we cannot account for them apart from some reference to the divine creative power, will, and purpose.

Human beings, as members of a particular species of mammalian primates, belong to this created world. Their morphological similarities to other animals are evident; so are their requirements for air, water, and food similar to the needs of many others. Individuals' bodies die as do those of all animals. Human beings belong to the earth and depend upon its natural environment for survival. They are not in essence otherworldly, even though their lives transcend matter and time.

There is a quality of human life to which the name "soul" or "spirit" or "personal ego" is given. It is related to the mind, to the brain's power of thought, but it is not the same thing as mind and brain. The cerebral cortex, brain, and nervous system exhibit functions, both cognitive and emotive, that to a limited degree are like functions perceived in some animals. But a theology of humanity asserts both the uniqueness of the human species and the uniqueness of each specimen, each person. This human character, unmatched among all living entities, is attributed to God.

The relationship of the individual human being to God, and of the whole human race to God, is a mystery more profound and more elusive of explanation than any phenomenon or operating activity in the universe. To be sure, this is an affirmation of faith, but not of "blind faith"; the evidences for it have been adduced from human experience for many centuries. In biblical faith the relationship is expressed concisely by the phrase "in the image of God."

Value

The intrinsic value of all human life and of each human life depends in principle, or implicitly, upon the relationship to God.

This does not mean that an individual values one's life only in respect to God; nor does it mean that placing the highest valuation on others' lives must arise only from such a faith. With or without acknowledging Christian faith, people may hold human life—the respect for inviolability, autonomy, and potential enhancement—in highest regard. But Christian faith holds this regard to be based in all instances on the human worth implied by "image of God," with all of the richness of that symbol.

Human Life

There is truth in the commonly expressed belief that "life is a gift of God." Some theologians are not content with the implications of this familiar idea. Often it can imply that life is just an animating force, only a vitalizing energy, imparted to both body and soul by God. This idea is ancient, attractive, and widely held. Such truth as there is in it is nevertheless deficient. Currently it is disputed by many biologists and physiologists who maintain an informed Christian faith. Why? The deficiency of the "gift of God" concept lies in its reticence about human responsibility. Does the Giver of the gift of life require anything of the recipient? Definitely. Life is not a "gift without strings attached." Christian faith emphasizes not only the autonomy and value of each one's life, but the theonomy and responsibility as well. This means that such moral imperatives as justice, truthfulness, and compassion are not virtues that were culturally invented and added onto human life; rather, they define what it means to be human. Just as the specifications for the many distinct characteristics of any living organism are encoded in their genes during exceedingly long times of adaptation and mutation, so the developed elements of humanness are encoded in what may be called man's moral history.

Life is more accurately thought of as a "loan" than as a "gift" from God. It is a quality held in trust, to be lived in freedom according to the known directives of God's will. For Christian faith, human life is inescapably a moral life, depending to be sure upon the physicochemical processes of the body but far transcending them in the dimensions of soul, spirit, and mind. From this premise arise numerous particular insights concerning the moral and immoral uses of life, and the purposeful goal of fulfilled personal life.

Responsibility in Face of Evil

While moral responsibility is expressed before God and to God, it is equally required in community with all other persons. Furthermore, it is extended to the world of nature, which in theological terms is better known as the creation.

Care for Creation

It is contrary to theology to think that the creation is static and immutable. Christian faith does not need, and is better without, a pseudoscientific theory of creationism, which attributes fixity to all life-forms and species. Rather, it asserts that creation is continuous, because the world and history have both purpose and future. A static view of all creation, or nature, is consistent with a deistic religion, according to which God is the Aristotelian "first cause" or an impersonal cosmic inventor and engineer. A Christian view is very different. It sees continuity among three kinds of activity—divine action, natural process, and human work. All three are continuing and changing. Creation is thus work in the process of becoming.

The stories concerning humanity and nature in Genesis are largely mythic in origin but, like many ancient myths, convey deep truth. The fact that the literary vehicle is mythical or legendary may obscure, but does not negate, the truth. The truth is the teaching of human responsibility before God and to God for the care and the use of the earth's resources and produce. Despite massive evidence in the past and present of irresponsible abuses of the earth, this insight and teaching remain valid. Ecological or environmental ethics for Christians should be seen as expressions of human stewardship. Because the human race is both a part of nature and also transcends nature, the moral imperatives of caring and using responsibly apply to human beings as objects of action as well as to nonhuman organisms and inert matter. Destructive exploitation of persons, animals, organisms, or inanimate things is essentially a violation of trust, and is the cause for moral condemnation.

Responsible stewardship is neither simple nor easy, however. It involves many contradictions, paradoxes, and moral dilemmas. The stories of Adam's Fall and Noah's reprieve—both referring to the whole race—illustrate the perplexities of the human condition. Both were given dominion over the earth—to care for it, to use its plants and animals for food, but without abusive exploitation. From this root grew the Hebrew laws of respect for all life and of preservation of the earth. Nevertheless, theology recognizes that throughout history the warnings against misuse, abuse, and exploitation have been ignored. The detrimental effects of such disregard are only now being fully seen and experienced. And one reason accounts for the abuse.

Sin

That reason is simply called "sin," an unfashionable and misconstrued concept. Sin is often thought to be mere human frailty, mortal limitation, or the failure of will to live up to ideal moral standards. Such meanings are superficial. Sin is the inexplicable, demonic contradiction within each reasoning and willing person between the will to be good and do good on the one hand, and the disposition toward egoism and exclusive self-interest on the other. Sin is self-deception even while it makes us try to deceive others. It is unwarranted confidence in one's own wisdom of decision and moral rectitude or self-sufficiency. Sin turns even the most ingenious of human achievements into instruments of injustice and maleficence.

Morever, sin is not a strictly individual fault. It belongs to human societies at large. Thus, it builds an environment that is scarcely friendly to human potential and well-being. Divested of the connotation of mere moralism, then, sin is the name for the historical human condition.

Given this weight of sin upon all human endeavor, manifest in self-love, malevolence, and moral impotence, Christian faith must struggle to explain, however inadequately, the presence of evil in the world. Why do things so often go wrong in human experiences of living despite all good intentions and efforts? Why does the perfectly good God permit the natural calamities, the humanly caused disasters, the massive injustices, the sufferings due to disease and starvation, the congenitally disabled persons, and all the melancholy catalog of manifest evil? The ultimate resolution of this puzzle—called theodicy, or the justification of faith in a good God—is beyond our understanding. It is literally an insoluble enigma. But the proximate and partly satisfying answer is cast in terms of human freedom, bestowed freely by God in creation. Sin and its mortal consequences are the risks required and the price paid for freedom; they are the unavoidable, but not insuperable, alternatives to our being amoral automata.

Suffering

There is suffering that seems cruel, destructive of life, and unbearable. There is suffering that seems grave only because we lack the courage or stamina to bear it. There is suffering accepted and endured out of respect or love for another person, for an idea, a cause, or a faith. So there are varieties of suffering: some are clearly evil, some are beneficial, some are morally ambiguous. The wisdom of Christian faith counsels neither resignation to suffering nor avoidance of it. It teaches patience and endurance where suffering is inevitable, and willingness to suffer when it is altruistic and vicarious. The prime symbol of faith is the cross, representing divine suffering in the person of Jesus Christ on behalf of humanity.

Distrust

Because of the pervasiveness of sin, Christians are justly suspicious of all pretenses of virtue and wisdom. Political power, popular panaceas, propaganda about programs of planned goodness for society are all held with a certain distrust. Who really knows what is good? Who *is* good? Only God is good. And the goodness attributed to all creation, including humanity, means just that it is suitable for the realizing of God's purposes.

This means that we must refrain from attributing absolute good to the relatively good beliefs, ideas, policies, and techniques of any human beings. This reserve is particularly required when the proferring of relative goods is conjoined with power. In human affairs power corrupts, whether the power be that of knowledge, technology, wealth, politics, religion, or a military machine.

In biblical faith the serious temptation and pitfall is idolatry—worshiping the creature rather than the Creator. In modern times, the idolatrous objects may be immaterial, such as ideas of racial superiority, ideological purity, sensuality, or even the all-sufficiency of scientific materialism. In political and social terms, therefore, Christian thought commends systems of checks and balances on the decisions and actions of persons, social institutions, commercial corporations, armies, and governments having inordinate power.

Uncertainty and Risk

The relative or imperfect good of human persons and institutions is matched by the partial knowledge they possess. In the totality of its historical experience, and especially during the past half-century, the human race has acquired a vast quantity of information, knowledge, and wisdom. Nonetheless, in respect of almost anything to which humans direct attention it can be said, "We know in part." Christian faith acknowledges this limitation, and still it encourages the quest for more knowledge. Its philosophical principle is that the world is real and thus knowable—it is not illusion. Christianity in Western civilization has stimulated and enabled scientific inquiry and contributed significantly to the rise of modern science. Regrettably, some Christian institutional authorities have resisted or suppressed the knowledge which in part was acquired precisely because of the encouragement given to scientists by the church's own doctrine.

The practical implications of this encouragement is that risks must be taken and limits acknowledged. Since "we cannot do anything against the truth, but only for the truth" (2 Cor. 13:8), the risk of freedom of scientific and philosophical inquiry must be accepted and promoted. Where the degree of uncertainty is high, so high is the need for risk taking. Yet, there are calculated, prudent risks as well as reckless ones. In investigation, research, and technical application where the probabilities of outcome are unknown, and where values and human lives are possibly put at risk, it is prudent to proceed with much caution. Such caution is in accord with both the encouragement to learn more of a subject and the protection of values and lives against inadvertent and irretrievable damage.

Another kind of uncertainty pertains to the effects upon one's own manner of life that are the consequences of one's own actions for the sake of others' benefit. The risk of following the ethical guides of Christian faith is that one may have to forfeit, or reject, some property or good condition that would bring pleasure and satisfaction at the cost of others' disadvantage or danger. Protestant ethics is often described in terms of the "theology of the cross" rather than the "theology of glory." This means that sincerity and faithfulness require taking paths of much resistance and performing actions of self-abnegation. The coming of Jesus Christ into Israel's history was an acceptance of the uncertainty and risk of his rejection, consequent suffering, and death. The clear lesson of Jesus' paradigmatic life and death is that deliberate risk to oneself, not to others, must be incurred if certain good objectives are to be gained for other people, whether few or many. Among such objectives today are the securing of defensible human rights, the supplying of basic needs for impoverished people, and providing the preventive and therapeutic health care which all must have.

Community

Christian faith is not an individualistic matter, as it is often caricatured to be. It is extremely personal, but not individualistic. The life of each person is seen in community—the community of family and friends, the community of the church, the wider social and civil communities. Insofar as the will of God for human conduct is known and enacted in these several communities, they provide the supporting contexts for mutual support, growth, and fulfillment. Where that will is unknown, ignored, violated, or rejected there are no longer communities but fragmented, impersonal societies.

The church community is distinctive for Christianity, of course. It necessarily takes sociological and institutional form, exhibiting its human faults and limitations. However, church community is believed by most Christians to have a nature, character, and purpose that transcend those of other associations and communities. Its members gather not only to worship and teach but to plan ways of helping other persons in their needs, of addressing problems of social justice and peace, and of sharing their faith by witness and example. In the dazzling complexity of contemporary cultures, shaped largely by scientific technology, there are few matters that stand outside the church's concern, however much they may be beyond its full competence. Hence the church's interest in the new science of genetic modification and its modesty in dealing with the inherent problems.

CORRELATING THEOLOGY WITH ISSUES IN GENETICS

Human Life—the Primary Criterion

The high value placed upon human life is obviously the primary criterion for judging the uses of genetic engineering and related biotechnologies. Concern for the integrity of life applies both to the individual and to the whole human race. The lives of one and all are valued for their intrinsic identity as created by God in his image. Their value is not determined by their scarcity, as with metals, gems, and food. Their worth as humans is not based upon their usefulness, as with some animals, machines, or other substances and products. Human value is intrinsic and inherent. In principle it is inviolable.

It may seem gratuitous for Christians, along with Jews, to claim that they have better reason than other people to honor each human being's integrity. But the decisive biblical doctrine clearly relates each human being—both body and soul together—to divine being. In Paul's words, "Your body is a temple of the Holy Spirit . . . ," and "Your bodies are members of Christ . . ." (1 Cor. 6:15, 19). In the theological understanding that informs Christian faith there is no clear line of distinction between unborn life and born life. At whatever stage of human development and existence, each and all human life is to be held in high respect. The application of this principle to dilemmas of life and death where lives come into conflict is notoriously a vexed and much-debated issue today. But the enhancement and fulfillment of each life remains the intended Christian purpose, however difficult to achieve.

Inevitable Modification

The natural, unmodified person as a unity of body, mind, and soul is not regarded by Christian thinking as immutable or normative. As people develop and mature, they are modified in mind and sensibility by numerous environmental, familial, and cultural influences. Education is modification; civilization requires it. Moreover, physiological modifications are inevitable due to diet, physical activity, disease, surgery, and accident. Modern surgical skill transplants into the body the organs and tissues taken from others, as well as chemicals and mechanical devices, to replace organs, bone, and tissue. In short, genetic engineering cannot be rejected on the ground of its being unnatural.

Autonomy, Responsibility, and Risk

The theological concept of a human person emphasizes both autonomy of will and decision as well as responsibility to God and to other persons. Neither autonomy nor responsibility overrides the other. Where the person's self is concerned, this means that a genetic intervention for purposes of either therapy or experiment requires the freely given consent of the person, in accord with presently accepted standards of informed consent. It also means that a person has responsibility for maintaining his or her own body and life in relation to family and friends and to God. In other words, one's life is not to be recklessly risked or needlessly sacrificed. Where the unborn, infants, or the mentally incompetent are concerned, the usual procedures (however uncertain) for surrogate decision should be followed.

Genetic engineering becomes a troubling issue whenever it might incur the risk of damaging the physical health, development or personal well-being of a human being. Such risk is most likely to occur inadvertently rather than deliberately. But intervention in any human organism for therapeutic purpose should not commence until sufficient evidence, both theoretical and empirical, can be adduced to give assurance that harmful effects will not ensue. This injunction presupposes the need for exhaustive experimenting on higher animals in the order of primates. (Harm to animals should likewise be kept to a minimum, since they too have a place in God's creation.)

Pharmaceuticals

The indirect therapeutic intervention by the use of antibodies, hormones, clotting factors, or other medicines, all of which will have been made by gene-splicing processes, poses no problems as long as their direct effects and side effects have been dependably plotted and found to be beneficial or innocuous.

Modifying Germ Cells

In principle there is no reason why a prohibition is needed against modifying the genetic content of germ cells (cells of ova and spermatozoa) as distinct from somatic cells. The initial intent would doubtless be therapeutic for the human organism in correcting a potentially debilitating genetic disease; and the secondary intent would be the protection of future progeny. In practice, however, it currently seems unlikely that sufficient knowledge is available even to theorize accurately about the long-term generational effects. Empirical data could be received, obviously, only from observations over many years. For the present, then, modifying germ cells should not be practiced at all.[3]

Embryonic Life

Although human life merits protection whether born or unborn, interventions in embryos and fetuses pose particular problems. There are proposals to practice gene-surgery upon embryonic cells *in vitro* prior to their being transferred to the prospective mother. These have been shown by recent research, using lower animal cells, to be probably feasible. Despite the successful birth of many babies following pregnancies that were induced by extracorporal fertilization, that process is still not free of moral ambiguities. *In vitro* fertilization, followed by gene surgery and implantation, should be practiced only under the strict protocols that focus all attention upon achieving childbirth for infertile parents.

169

Gene therapy procedures affecting only the somatic cells of developing fetuses can be judged in theory in the same way as recent advances in fetal surgery. They enhance the possibilities of healthy life after birth and thus reduce, or obviate, parental inclination to deny the fetus birth in order to avoid a predictably unhealthy life.

Eugenics

Programs for "positive" eugenics have been advocated, debated, and discredited in the past. Now their advocates can include genetic modification as a further factor beyond genetic counseling and screening. However, the arguments against public eugenic programs have been, and still remain, persuasive when based upon the Christian belief about humanity.[4]

Animals and Plants

The preceding discussions of theological reasons for valuing human life indicate why distinctions of moral judgment are made between applications of genetic technique to human beings and to animals and plants. The doctrine of creation emphasizes the primacy of human value, which is served by responsible uses of animals and plants. That is, animal husbandry for food, hides, and chemicals—and agriculture as well—may surely be improved by genetic science. But inhumane, brutal treatment of animals and imprudent, wasteful uses of agricultural products are condemned. The still-unknown effects of genetic modification of plants upon ecosystems and upon the plants' resistance to diseases await adequate research and commend caution.

Crossing Species Barriers

The breeding of novel hybrids by crossing the barriers of species has proved already to be beneficial to humanity where plants for food and fiber are concerned. It becomes more and more problematical in respect to animal species of ascending orders of sentiency and consciousness. There are complicated ecological reasons as well as theological reasons for such judgment. But any dispute must disappear when the human species is concerned. Research in this area is morally illicit and repugnant.[5]

Social, Economic, and
Political Implications

Christian theology and ethics have much to say about social welfare, order, and justice; so discussions about genetic engineering are not confined to effects upon the individuals concerned. Many perplexing problems of a social character are being identified. These often involve economic, ecological, and political factors of highest importance. Without entering into detailed consideration of these issues, certain theological perceptions and moral judgments can here be briefly suggested as pertinent to them and correlative to the Protestant Christian doctrines just defined:

1. Truth-telling is a virtue integral to human value. It can be put at risk, however, by the burgeoning science of genetic manipulation. It must be honored with full sincerity, so that persons directly or indirectly affected by genetic science are neither misled by false hopes nor exploited and harmed.

2. The patenting of new forms of cellular life, already approved in one case by the United States Supreme Court, remains a problematical and potentially dangerous policy.

3. Many agricultural and industrial uses of genetic science appear to promise benefits to society, for example in mining, food production, and the making of pharmaceuticals. But the morally ambiguous implications of commercialization are also evident and in need of sober examination, for example with respect to exploitation of scientific research and scientists for corporate profit making, keeping prices of medicines and pharmaceuticals at unwarranted levels, maintaining in matters of research a secrecy which is detrimental to science, and evading safety regulations in one country by going to an unregulated country for production and marketing.

4. Pathogenic dangers have been thoroughly discussed, and some initial fears have been allayed; but a wholly laissez-faire policy for laboratories and industries is not justified. Regulations that protect workers as well as the general society are still in order, as the National Institutes of Health maintain. The Recombinant-DNA Advisory Committee of the NIH recognizes that

within and beyond the laboratory and industry are wider areas where novel and uncontrollable organisms can threaten public health and safety; but its powers of enforcement are small.[6]

5. Bacteriological herbicides and "hominicides" intended for military use should be outlawed. The fact that microbiological weaponry may be ultimately less lethal than thermonuclear weapons does not render them acceptable.

6. The concentration of power in the minds and hands of genetic scientists, industrialists, and militaristic politicians is a cause for grave concern. The immoral characters in comic books and films, monsters who are willing to kill masses of people for political, economic, or egomaniac reasons, do not dwell in fictional stories only. They have recently been with us in the world and have not departed. However much comfort may be found in the it-can't-happen-here attitude, a constant vigilance must be maintained against the catastrophic exploitation of genetic powers.

THE FOCUS ON PURPOSE

Although scientists, legislators, public officials, and other concerned persons may receive with appreciation and favor the comment of religious ethicists upon the whole cluster of issues surrounding genetic technology, such comments can pose a serious question: Do the judgments about applied genetics which rest upon these religious doctrines and insights differ substantially from those which are declared to have been reached without benefit of clergy or divinity? Answers from several leading religious scholars are diverse. Ostensibly, the same practical positions with respect to particular problems can be reached either by resort to the illuminations of revealed truth or by the thoughtful analysis of relevant data. Attitudes, motivations, expectations, and methods of intellectual analysis clearly differ among people who seek and find the same solutions.

One objective of the life sciences in both research and application is the relief and reducing of disease, suffering, and adverse modes of living that hinder the realization of life's good purposes. Such an objective was also central to the ministry of Jesus Christ among people who were impoverished, sick, and sorely oppressed. The very axis of Christian faith is the perception that the suffering that accompanies sin, perversity, and evil in society can be overcome by the divine sharing of it. The main trust of the cross in Christian faith thus appears to agree with the purpose of such applied scientific technique as genetic manipulation. Both are directed against the kind of negativities that injure or destroy life and its goodness. Those are sincere and worthy intentions. Yet, as we know from much experience, the best of intentions can lead to the most corrupt consequences. This generation's technical achievements in industry, energy, medicine, and biology may become the nemeses—or the great blessings—of coming generations.

Because of the high valuation of each one's mortal life, biblically informed faith commits people to assist one another throughout human society to enjoy healthful and rewarding living. This is the motivation for prophetic and constructive striving for justice and opportunity on behalf of all who are weak, disadvantaged, and exploited. It is also the reason why scientific techniques which can affect both the organic cells of human beings and their environment are matters of religious concern. Indeed, the Bible links the renewal and fulfillment of life for human beings to the transformation of the whole creation.

NOTES

WHERE THERE'S HOPE THERE'S LIFE

1. Sigmund Freud, *Civilization and Its Discontents*, trans. James Strachey (New York: W. W. Norton & Co., 1962), 22–23.

2. Thomas Gray, "ELEGY written in a COUNTRY CHURCH YARD," as the 1768 first edition gave the title.

3. T. S. Eliot, "Choruses from 'The Rock,'" *Collected Poems, 1909–1962* (New York: Harcourt Brace Jovanovich, Inc., 1963), 184.

4. James C. Mohr's well-researched study reveals why there was a general sense of repugnance toward abortion in nineteenth-century America; see *Abortion in America* (New York: Oxford University Press, 1978).

5. Fredric Wertham in *A Sign for Cain* (New York: Macmillan Co., 1966), 161, reveals that the serious proposal for the elimination of all *Lebensunwerten* in Germany was made as early as 1920 by Alfred Hoche, a prominent psychiatrist, and Karl Binding, a lawyer, in their book, *The Destruction of Life Devoid of Value*. While Adolf Hitler put the monstrous theory into practice, he did not invent it; he merely appropriated what was already becoming morally acceptable, a fact that makes him no less culpable, of course. In this important study of the pathology of violence the author fails, however, to mention the wanton killings under Josef Stalin in the Soviet Union, for whom political opponents too were unworthy of life.

6. According to the research team of Japanese Dr. Yokichi Hayasaka, reporting on "Japan's 22 Year Experience with a Liberal Abortion Law" (1970), the legislation of the Eugenic Protection Law (1948 and 1952) was intended to prevent the birth of "inferior descendants" and also to protect the life and health of the mother; but limiting population as such was not given as a rationale for it. The report is printed in *Hearing before the Subcommittee on Constitutional Amendments of the Committee on the Judiciary, United States Senate* (Washington, D.C.: Government Printing Office, 1976), 663–93.

7. Marvin Kohl, ed., *Infanticide and the Value of Life* (Buffalo: Prometheus Books, 1978).

8. The transfer of the method of medical triage—separating patients according to need for treatment—to the situation of malnutrition and

starvation in drought-stricken or overpopulated countries has been vigorously advocated by Garrett Hardin. His provocative article "Lifeboat Ethics: The Case against Helping the Poor," *Psychology Today* (September 1974), started a passionate debate, which is constructively discussed by Hardin and others in *Lifeboat Ethics*, ed. George R. Lucas, Jr., and Thomas Ogletree (New York: Harper & Row, 1976).

9. A lively, often acrimonious, debate among anthropologists concerning the sources and causes of aggression and violent intraspecies killing by human beings has been occasioned largely by the writings of Konrad Lorenz and his student Irenaeus Eibl-Eibesfeldt. Robert Ardrey and Desmond Morris have appropriated the more pessimistic of the anthropological data and popularized the notion that human beings are by nature just "naked apes" in "the human zoo." The cynical appraisal of human behavior as basically selfish and aggressive, even as genetically determined, is challenged by experts in a variety of fields, including human paleontology, sociobiology, psychology, philosophy, and theology. A good discussion of the serious problem is found in Eibl-Eibesfeldt, *The Biology of Peace and War*, trans. Eric Mosbacher (New York: Viking Press, 1979), and in Hans Schwarz, *Our Cosmic Journey* (Minneapolis: Augsburg Publishing House, 1977).

10. Elizabeth Kübler-Ross, *On Death and Dying* (New York: Macmillan Co., 1969).

LIFE, THE GREAT PRESUPPOSITION STILL UNDEFINED

1. *Encyclopaedia Britannica*, 15th ed., Micropaedia, s.v. "life."

2. Philip Handler, ed., *Biology and the Future of Man* (New York: Oxford University Press, 1970), 498.

3. Hans Jonas, *The Phenomenon of Life* (New York: Harper & Row, 1966), 7–8.

4. Ibid., 9.

5. Johann Gottlieb Fichte, *Die Bestimmung des Menschen*, 1800, cited by Karl Barth in vol. 3, part 2 of *Church Dogmatics*, trans. by Harold Knight, et al. (Edinburgh: T. & T. Clark, 1960), 102.

6. Albert Schweitzer, *Out of My Life and Thought*, trans. C. T. Campion (New York: Henry Holt Co., 1937), 156. See also Gerald McKnight, *Verdict on Schweitzer* (New York: John Day, 1964), 196.

7. Albert Schweitzer, *Kultur und Ethik* (Munich: Biederstein Verlag, 1948), 211.

8. Albert Schweitzer, *Indian Thought and Its Developments*, trans. C. E. B. Russell (London: Hodder & Stoughton, 1936), 79.

9. Ibid., 83.

10. Marjorie Grene rightly stresses the important distinction between

telos and *entelecheia* as used by Aristotle and the divine purpose of fulfillment which is conveyed by the teleological words of biblical faith. She writes: "There is absolutely no question of any kind of 'purpose' here, either man's or God's. To suppose otherwise is to introduce a Judaeo-Christian confusion of which Aristotle must be entirely acquitted." *The Understanding of Nature* (Dordrecht and Boston: D. Reidel Publishing Co., 1974), 77. Since the word "teleological" usually implies the concept of purpose, either philosophical or theological, Ernst Mayr suggests another word, "teleonomy," which pertains only to the indispensable modes of behavior by which the organism functions toward the simple goal of survival. "Teleological and Teleonomic: A New Analysis," in *Methodological and Historical Essays in the Natural and Social Sciences: Proceedings of the Boston Colloquium for the Philosophy of Science, 1969–1972*, Boston Studies in the Philosophy of Science, vol. XIV., ed. Robert S. Cohen and Marx W. Wartofsky (Dordrecht: D. Reidel Publishing Co., 1974), 97–117.

11. Lucretius, *On the Nature of Things*, in vol. 12 of *Great Books of the Western World* (Chicago: Encyclopaedia Britannica, 1952), 26.

12. Jonas, *Phenomenon of Life*, 8.

13. Ibid., 11.

14. Immanuel Kant, *The Critique of Teleological Judgement* in vol. 42 of *Great Books of the Western World* (Chicago: Encyclopaedia Britannica, 1952), 567.

15. C. U. M. Smith, *The Problem of Life* (New York and Toronto: John Wiley & Sons, 1976), 30. This book is a superb survey of biology and philosophy.

16. See Stanley L. Jaki, *The Road of Science and the Ways of God* (Chicago: University of Chicago Press, 1978), chaps. 2–3.

17. René Descartes, *Discourse on the Method of Rightly Conducting the Reason*, in vol. 31 of *Great Books of the Western World* (Chicago: Encyclopaedia Britannica, 1952), 59.

18. Ibid., 60.

19. John Wesley, sermon on "The Fall of Man," in vol. 6 of *The Works of John Wesley* (Grand Rapids: Zondervan Publishing House, reprint of 1872 ed.), 219.

20. Kant, *Critique of Teleological Judgement*, 578.

21. Ibid., 561.

22. Ibid., 574, 576.

23. Among the many excellent histories of the biological sciences, see William Coleman, *Biology in the Nineteenth Century* (New York and Toronto: John Wiley & Sons, 1971). A recent critical discussion of the materialist-vitalist debate is in Charles Birch and John B. Cobb, Jr., *The Liberation of Life* (Cambridge: Cambridge University Press, 1981), chap. 3.

24. Darwin is quoted in *Encyclopaedia Britannica*, 14th ed., s. v. "Darwin."

25. Quoted by Smith, *Problem of Life*, 252.

26. Marjorie Grene, *Approaches to a Philosophical Biology* (New York: Basic Books, 1965), 59.

27. Gaylord G. Simpson, *The Meaning of Evolution* (New York: Oxford University Press, 1950), 344.

28. Smith, *Problem of Life*, xvi.

29. A. R. Peacocke, "The Molecular Organization of Life" in *Biology and Personality*, ed. Ian T. Ramsey (Oxford: Basil Blackwell & Mott, 1965), 18. Italics added.

30. Henry Drummond, *Natural Law in the Spiritual World* (New York: Lovell, 1981), 64.

31. Hans Driesch, *The Problem of Individuality* (London: Macmillan & Co., 1914), 19.

32. Hans Driesch, *The Science and Philosophy of the Organism* (London: A. & C. Black, 1908), 144.

33. Driesch, *Problem of Individuality*, 38.

34. So Marjorie Grene interprets Driesch and Plessner, *Approaches to a Philosophical Biology*, 69.

35. Henri Bergson, *Creative Evolution*, trans. Arthur Mitchell (New York: Henry Holt & Co., 1924), 42.

36. Bertrand Russell, *History of Western Philosophy* (London: George Allen & Unwin, Ltd., 1961), 757.

37. Ibid., 762.

38. Ibid., 764.

39. George Bernard Shaw, *Nine Plays* (New York: Dodd, Mead & Co., 1944), 617–37.

40. Coleman, *Biology in the Nineteenth Century*, 11.

41. Gunther S. Stent, *Paradoxes of Progress* (San Francisco: W. H. Freeman Co., 1978), 116. Stent opposes vitalism in *The Molecular Biology of Bacterial Viruses* (San Francisco: W. H. Freeman Co., 1963).

42. Stent, *Paradoxes of Progress*, 116. See Francis J. Crick, *Of Molecules and Men* (Seattle: University of Washington, 1966), 26. Some other representative statements in refutation of any kind of vitalistic theories are the following:

> All these theories, vitalist, finalist, or both, involved some degree of abandonment of causalism. They did not explain evolution, but claimed that it is inexplicable and then gave a name to its inexplicability, *élan vital* (Bergson), "cellular consciousness" (Buis, under the pseudonym "Pierre Jean"), "aristogenesis" (Osborne), "nomogenesis" (Berg), "holism" (Smuts), "entelechy" (Driesch), "telefinalism" (du Noüy), "the Principle of Organization" (Sinnott), "Omega"

(Teilhard)—the list could be greatly extended. . . . But the fact that the history of life is flatly inconsistent with their basic propositions does warrant the conclusion that vitalism and finalism are untenable. (Gaylord G. Simpson, *The Meaning of Evolution*, 273–74)

To the mechanist, all biological events require explanation in physical and chemical terms, and hence *everything* arouses surprise and interest. Probing questions are asked, nothing is taken for granted, and the result is progress. The vitalist is left in his armchair, contentedly pondering the occult . . . Nothing so far discovered warrants the view that biochemical events will *never* be totally explained in physiochemical terms. (William S. Beck, *Modern Science and the Nature of Life* [New York: Harcourt, Brace and Co., 1957], 137–38.)

43. Jacques Monod, *Chance and Necessity*, trans. Austryn Wainhouse (New York: Vintage Books, 1971), 25–32.

44. Ibid., 116. Italics original. Ernst Mayr is just as adamant as Monod in rejecting any theory that suggests a life force. He even declares that "life" itself has no reality in itself: "Life is simply the reification of the processes of living. . . . There is no such thing as an independent 'life' in a living organism." Mayr judges that such writers as Hans Jonas and Marjorie Grene are too lenient toward the philosophical view of life as having a reality of its own. *The Growth of Biological Thought* (Cambridge: Harvard University Press, 1982), 74f.

45. John B. Habgood, *Religion and Science* (London: Hodder & Stoughton, 1964/1972), 58. A complete history of vitalistic thinking up to the 1930s was writted by L. Richmond Wheeler, *Vitalism: Its History and Validity* (London: H. F. & G. Witherby, 1939). Although he follows closely the book of Hans Driesch, *History and Theory of Vitalism* (London: Macmillan & Co., 1914), Wheeler discusses mainly the British and French scientists. The obvious deficiency of his book is the inevitable lack of scientific information about microbiology and genetics. Reading it, one is made aware of the huge difference that the decoding of the DNA molecule has made in thinking about life. Wheeler's concluding personal statement nevertheless remains germane:

As I see it, modern vitalism stands for broad views in biology, accepting all that other branches of science can offer but employing, where necessary, distinctive, fundamental, concepts not derivable from the material of inorganic science.(262)

The book of Rainer Schubert-Soldern of Vienna, *Mechanism and Vitalism*, trans. C. E. Robin (Notre Dame, Ind.: University of Notre Dame Press, 1962) offers a more penetrating analysis of the question, yet remains critically friendly to the intention of the vitalists; it refers almost exclusively to German scientific writers. Finally, the British zoologist Alister Hardy in *The Living Stream* (New York: Harper & Row, 1965) expresses tentativeness toward both mechanism and vitalism, but also offers hope for their eventual resolution or transcendence by means of knowledge yet to be gained in humanity's rapidly advancing intellectual quest:

> I am not a vitalist in the old-fashioned sense of the word. I fully expect that the whole of an animal's bodily mechanism will be resolved in terms of biophysics and biochemistry; but I am not a materialist in that I am blind to the reality of consciousness in the organic world. (34)

Hardy expands his views in *The Biology of God* (London: Jonathan Cape, 1975). A similar position is developed by H. Sachsse, *Die Erkenntnis des Lebendigen* (Braunschweig: Vieweg, 1968), 5; as well as Hoimar von Ditfurth, *The Origins of Life*, trans. Peter Heinegg (San Francisco: Harper & Row, 1981), 53.

46. Theodosius Dobzhansky, *Genetics of the Evolutionary Process* (New York: Columbia University Press, 1970), 1.

47. Carl Sagan in *Encyclopaedia Britannica*, 15th ed., Macropaedia, s. v. "life."

RECOVERING THE HEBRAIC INSIGHT

1. The differing possibilities for relating the knowledge gained through natural science to that of religious faith are discussed in my book, *Science and Our Troubled Conscience* (Philadelphia: Fortress Press, 1980), 43–56. The five relationships are: (1) mutual exclusion of separate realities; (2) mutual exclusion, though dealing with the same realities; (3) interacting approaches to the same realities; (4) mutual interaction; and (5) integration by unification or absorption. It is the fourth type that I consider most appropriate for persons of open mind, whether their knowledge and mode of thinking is determined mainly by natural science or by faith and theology. It may more accurately be called "dialectical interaction" in view of the give and take of information and wisdom which are involved.

2. Michael Landmann, *Philosophical Anthropology*, trans. David J. Parent (Philadelphia: Westminster Press, 1974), 73.

3. Immanuel Jakobovits, *Jewish Medical Ethics* (New York: Bloch Publishing Co., 1959), xxii.

4. Hans Jonas, *The Phenomenon of Life* (New York: Harper & Row, 1966), 13.

5. C. A. van Peursen, *Body, Soul, Spirit: A Survey of the Body-Mind Problem*, trans. Hubert H. Hoskins (London: Oxford University Press, 1966), 49.

6. Aristotle, "On the Soul," in vol. 8 of *Great Books of the Western World* (Chicago: University of Chicago, 1952), 644. The ostensible compatibility of Aristotle's view of the soul-body unity with that of the Bible accounts in large measure for the eventual adoption of his philosophy by medieval theologians of Western Europe. Of this notion of inseparability of soul and body in the human person, there is clarity in Carsten Johnsen's statement:

> The soul is the act of the living body (the *entelechy* of the living body). It is that man, as far as he really exists at all—as a living being. It is, in fact—according to Aristotle—just the intimate union between form and matter which constitutes the concrete substance of things and makes up the reality of all beings, such as we know them in actual life. And in that reality the form (soul) is never separated from the matter (body).

Johnsen's well-informed and spirited critique of dualistic anthropology, *Man—the Indivisible* (Oslo: Universitetsforlaget, 1971), from page 157 of which the quotation is drawn, accords congenially with the present study of Greek and Hebraic-Christian concepts of life.

7. A. E. Taylor in *Encyclopaedia Britannica*, 14th ed., s.v. "Plato."

8. Rudolf Bultmann in vol. 2 of *Theological Dictionary of the New Testament*, ed. Gerhard Kittel, trans. Geoffrey W. Bromiley (Grand Rapids: W. B. Eerdmans, 1964), s.v. "ZAŌ." The same text appears in vol. 5 of *Bible Key Words* (New York: Harper & Row, 1963), 52–55.

9. John Calvin, *Institutes of the Christian Religion*, trans. Henry Beveridge (London: James Clarke & Co., 1949), Book I, xv. 2, 160.

10. Cyril of Jerusalem, *The Catechetical Lectures*, trans. Mr. Church of Oriel College (Oxford: J. H. Parker, 1845), 42, 44.

11. Richard M. Zaner in *Encyclopedia of Bioethics*, ed. Warren T. Reich (New York: Free Press, 1978), s.v. "embodiment," vol. I, 365.

12. Bultmann, *Bible Key Words*, 14–19.

13. Marjorie Grene, *Approaches to Philosophical Biology* (New York: Basic Books, 1968), 177.

14. Hans Küng, *Signposts for the Future* (New York: Doubleday & Co., 1978), 69. Another accounting for the artist's fascination with the crucifix is stated by one of the editors of his works, who writes of Chagall's "opinion, often affirmed, that Christ is the highest expression of humanity." Bernard Dorival, *Donation Marc et Valentin Chagall* (Paris: Louvre, 1967), 4.

15. Otto Piper in *The Interpreter's Dictionary of the Bible* (New York: Abingdon Press, 1962), s.v. "life."

16. Gerhard Dautzenberg, *Sein Leben Bewahren* (Munich: Kösel Verlag, 1966), 28.

17. Hans-Walter Wolff, *Anthropology of the Old Testament*, trans.

Margaret Kohl (Philadelphia: Fortress Press, 1974), 10–20. See also Dautzenberg, *Sein Leben Bewahren*, 11–30, and Johannes Pedersen, *Israel*, vol. 1 (Copenhagen: Branner og Korch, 1926), 110, 152, 156, 165.

18. C. U. M. Smith, *The Problem of Life* (New York and Toronto: John Wiley & Sons, 1976), 109.

19. Wolff, *Anthropology of the Old Testament*, 60. Pedersen, *Israel*, 104, 123. Concerning the cultic, sacrificial laws on blood see Roland de Vaux, *Ancient Israel*, trans. John McHugh (New York: McGraw-Hill, 1961), 419.

20. Aristotle, "On the Parts of Animals," in vol. 9 of *Great Books of the Western World*, 194.

21. Wolff, *Anthropology of the Old Testament*, 40.

22. Ibid., 55.

23. Van Peursen, *Body, Soul, Spirit*, 100.

24. Edmond Jacob in *Theological Dictionary of the New Testament*, ed. Gerhard Kittel, trans. Geoffrey W. Bromiley (Grand Rapids: W. B. Eerdmans, 1974), s.v. "psuchē."

25. T. S. Eliot, "Choruses from 'The Rock,'" in *Collected Poems, 1909–1962* (New York: Harcourt Brace Jovanovich, 1963), 188.

26. Wolff, *Anthropology of the Old Testament*, 62.

27. For excellent surveys of interpretations of *imago Dei* see David Cairns, *The Image of God in Man* (New York: Philosophical Library, 1953); and James M. Childs, Jr., *Christian Anthropology and Ethics* (Philadelphia: Fortress Press, 1978), chaps. 2, 4, with notes.

28. Karl Barth, *Church Dogmatics*, trans. Geoffrey W. Bromiley (Edinburgh: T. & T. Clark, 1958), vol. 3, part 1, 183ff.

29. Martin Buber, *I and Thou*, trans. Ronald Gregor Smith (New York: Charles Scribner's Sons, 1958).

30. Edward O. Wilson's lecture, "The Social Instinct," *Bulletin of the American Academy of Arts and Sciences* 30 (October 1976): 11–25. Wilson, the eminent zoologist and entomologist, expands his thesis of sociobiology in the much-debated book, *On Human Nature* (Cambridge: Harvard University Press, 1978). Critical discussion of the anthropological and philosophical implications of the thesis was held with Wilson at a symposium in 1979. These papers, including my own response as a theologian, are published in *Zygon* 15:3–4 (September and December 1980).

31. Adolf Portmann, "Biology and the Phenomenon of the Spiritual," *Spirit and Nature: Papers from the Eranos Yearbook* (New York: Pantheon Books, 1954), 355.

32. Grene, *Approaches to Philosophical Biology*, 81.

33. Portmann, "Biology and the Phenomenon of the Spiritual," 357.

34. Blaise Pascal, *Pensées*, trans. W. F. Potter (New York: Random House Modern Library, 1941), 81. Pascal's *pari*, or wager, is well in-

terpreted by Roger Hazelton, *Pascal, the Genius of His Thought* (Philadelphia: Westminster Press, 1974), 145–52; and Romano Guardini, *Pascal for Our Time*, trans. Brian Thompson (New York: Herder & Herder, 1966), 146f.

THREE DIMENSIONS OF ONE LIFE

1. Will Herberg, *Judaism and Modern Man* (New York: Meridian Books, 1960), 229.

2. Edmond Jacob in *Theological Dictionary of the New Testament*, ed. Gerhard Kittel, trans. G. W. Bromiley (Grand Rapids: W. B. Eerdmans, 1974), s.v. "psuchē."

3. Various Christian writers, who both affirm the resurrection of Jesus as a matter of faith and seek intelligible ways of conceiving how it happened, have been encouraged by two areas of modern research—physical theory and parapsychology. Leslie D. Weatherhead, a famous London preacher, advanced a hypothesis which he found compelling and consistent with Christian theology: "Could the spirit of Christ act upon His body in such a way as to alter the molecular speed and make the body take gaseous form in an unusually short time?" Weatherhead evades the problem of the physical substance of Jesus' risen body: "Further, if the particles of His flesh were still being used by Him in His risen body, we would have only postponed a difficulty and failed to answer the question, 'What *ultimately* happened to the fleshly body of Christ?'. . . . For my own part, I think that in the tomb He finished finally with matter as the medium of His manifestations and used thereafter what is technically an apparitional form, a form which does not deny His real presence or fail to stimulate the brain-centres of the percipient in the same way and to the same degree as does matter." *The Manner of the Resurrection* (New York: Abingdon Press, 1959), 52, 64–65.

4. See Rudolf Bultmann in *The Theological Dictionary of the New Testament*, s.v. "zaō" (and the same in Bultmann, *Bible Key Words*). See chap. 3, n. 8.

5. Aristotle, *Nicomachean Ethics*: *Great Books of the Western World*, vol. 9 (Chicago: University of Chicago, 1952), I:5, 1095b, 340–341.

6. Ibid., X:7, 1178a, 432. See Bultmann, *Bible Key Words*, 5:II, 24.

7. John Hick, *Death and Eternal Life* (New York: Harper & Row, 1976), 45.

8. The three-part classification of the meaning of *psuchē* is a defensible variation of the more detailed scheme of classes and subclasses of usage which is followed in *A Greek-English Lexicon of the New Testament*, the translation and adaptation of Walter Bauer's German work

by W. F. Arndt and E. W. Gingrich (Chicago: University of Chicago, 1957), 901–2.

9. Dautzenberg, *Sein Leben Bewahren*, 57.

10. Eduard Schweizer in *Theological Dictionary of the New Testament*, s.v. "psuchē."

11. Karl Barth, *Church Dogmatics*, vol. 3, part 2, trans. G. W. Bromiley (Edinburgh: T. & T. Clark, 1960), 379.

12. Vincent Taylor, *The Gospel According to St. Mark* (London: Macmillan & Co., 1952), 282.

13. Dautzenberg, *Sein Leben Bewahren*, 57, 66.

14. Schweizer, *Theological Dictionary of the New Testament*, s.v. "psuchē."

15. Few questions have become so vexing today as the defining of "humanhood" and thus drawing the line between intrinsically protectible and defenseless life. This is the crucial issue in the field of bioethics and in medical ethics, affecting the life or death of unborn babies, genetically impaired neonates, those severely retarded mentally, and those in prolonged and apparently irretrievable unconsciousness. Although the New Testament says nothing specifically about the degrees of humanhood, or its absence, its implicit concepts of life can help us think through the issues presented in modern society by medical technology.

16. Bultmann, *Bible Key Words*, vol. 5, II, 47, 52.

17. Several passages illustrate how the verb *zaō*, "I live," refers to dimensions of life which we would designate *psuchē* rather than *zōē*, among them being (where the Revised Standard Version gives the English form of the Greek): (a) Physical life in contrast to death: Rom. 7:2, 3; 14:8; 2 Cor. 4:11; Luke 15:24; Matt. 9:18. (b) Life in the flesh: Gal. 2:20; Col. 2:20; Acts 17:28. (c) Life dependent on bread: Luke 4:4.

18. Augustine cited by Barth, *Church Dogmatics*, 153.

19. Rudolph Bultmann, *The Gospel of John*, trans. G. R. Beasley-Murray (Philadelphia: Westminster Press, 1971), 39, n. 3. Another respected and exacting scholar who believes this wording is preferable, and perhaps originally intended by John, is Raymond E. Brown, *The Gospel According to John*, Anchor Bible Series (Garden City, N.Y.: Doubleday & Co., 1966), 6. Brown explains that the ancient church fathers generally accepted Jerome's version; but the alternate, ". . . without him was not anything made that was made," was adopted for apologetic purposes, against Arians and dualists who did not believe the Christian interpretation of the creation as matter made by the transcendent God.

20. C. H. Dodd, *The Interpretation of the Fourth Gospel* (Cambridge: Cambridge University Press, 1960), 147.

21. Rudolf Schnackenburg, *The Gospel According to John*, trans. Kevin Smyth (New York: Herder & Herder, 1968), 242. Schnackenburg accepts the wording, "In him was life, and the life was the light of men."

22. See Raymond E. Brown, "The *Ego Eimi* ("I am") Passages in the Fourth Gospel," in *A Companion to John*, ed. Michael J. Taylor (New York: Alba House, 1977), 117–25. A more technical treatment is Eduard Schweizer, *EGO EIMI* (*Forschungen zur Religion und Literatur des Alten und Neuen Testaments*) (Göttingen: Vandenhoeck und Ruprecht, 1939). A short one is found in Hans Conzelmann, *An Outline of the Theology of the New Testament*, trans. John Bowden (New York: Harper & Row, 1969), 349–52.

23. See Hans Jonas, *The Gnostic Religion* (Boston: Beacon Press, 1963); Elaine H. Pagels, *The Gnostic Paul* (Philadelphia: Fortress Press, 1975); idem, *The Gnostic Gospels* (New York: Random House, 1979).

24. Franz Mussner, *ZŌĒ die Anschauung vom "Leben" im Vierten Evangelium* (Munich: E. Zink, 1952), 73.

25. Brown, "*Ego Eimi*," 7, 506.

26. C. F. D. Moule, "The Meaning of 'Life' in the Gospel and Epistles of John," *Theology* 78:657 (March 1975): 122–23.

27. Bultmann, *Bible Key Words*, vol. 5, II, 74–75.

A WORKABLE DEFINITION OF LIFE

1. Peter Singer, *Practical Ethics* (Cambridge: Cambridge University Press, 1979), 76. The reductionist view of human life, according to which human beings are "nothing but animals," is not shared by all scientists and philosophers who deny any transcendent or metaphysical dimension of humanity. Stephen Jay Gould, an evolutionary biologist of wide reputation, attributes the manifest eminence of human life on the earth to neither genetic uniqueness nor divine purpose but to "cultural evolution." "We are inextricably part of nature," he writes, "but human uniqueness is not negated thereby. 'Nothing but' an animal is as fallacious a statement as 'created in God's own image.' It is not mere hubris to argue that Homo sapiens is special in some sense—for each species is unique in its own way; shall we judge among the dance of the bees, the song of the humpback whale, and human intelligence?" *The Mismeasure of Man* (New York: W. W. Norton & Co., 1981), 324.

2. Raymond A. Moody, *Life after Life* (New York: Bantam Books, 1975), has been one of the most widely read accounts of instances in which death was actually experienced and then remembered by those who survived by resuscitation. The acknowledged leader in the field of thanatology, Elisabeth Kübler-Ross, wrote in the foreword that Moody's book appeared just as she herself was becoming convinced of the reality of these experiences.

3. *Encyclopaedia of Judaica*, vol. 11, (Jerusalem: Macmillan, 1971), 235.

4. Paul Tillich, *Systematic Theology*, vol. 3 (Chicago: University of Chicago Press, 1963), 12.

5. T. S. Eliot, "Choruses from 'The Rock,'" in *Collected Poems, 1909–1962* (New York: Harcourt Brace Jovanovich, 1963), 179.

6. Tillich, *Systematic Theology*, 12.

7. Karl Barth, *Church Dogmatics*, vol. 3, part 2, trans. Harold Knight et al., (Edinburgh: T. & T. Clark, 1960), 323–24.

8. Pierre Teilhard de Chardin, *The Phenomenon of Man*, trans. Bernard Wall (London: William Collins Sons, 1959), 165.

9. Tillich, *Systematic Theology*, 36.

10. George Fradier, *About the quality of life* (Paris: UNESCO, 1976), 8.

11. *The Boston Globe* (November 8, 1976), 5.

12. Anthony Shaw, "Defining the Quality of Life," *The Hastings Center Report* (Hastings-on-Hudson, N.Y.), vol. 7, no. 5 (October 1977), 11.

13. Sissela Bok, "Who Shall Count as a Human Being?" in *Abortion: Pro and Con*, ed. R. Perkins (Cambridge: Schenckman, 1974), 98.

14. Edward Shils, "The Sanctity of Life," in *Life or Death, Ethics and Options*, ed. D. H. Labby (Seattle: University of Washington Press, 1968), 9.

15. Ibid., 15.

16. Ibid., 17. Kurt Baier expresses a view similar to Shils's in "Technology and the Sanctity of Life," in *Ethics and Problems of the 21st Century*, ed. K. M. Sayre and K. E. Goodpaster (South Bend, Ind.: University of Notre Dame Press, 1979), 162–65.

17. Daniel Callahan, *Abortion: Law, Choice and Morality* (New York: Macmillan Co., 1970), 306–48. A revised, shortened form of this important essay is found in a book most pertinent to this study, *Updating Life and Death*, ed. Donald R. Cutler (Boston: Beacon Press, 1968), 181–223.

18. William K. Frankena, "The Ethics of Respect for Life," in *Respect for Life* (Baltimore: Johns Hopkins University Press, 1976), 24–62.

19. Callahan, *Abortion*, 308. (In *Updating Life and Death*, 184.)

20. Frankena, "Ethics of Respect for Life," 32.

21. Ibid., 44.

22. Ibid., 54.

23. Callahan, *Abortion*, 319. (In *Updating Life and Death*, 194).

24. Karl Barth, *Church Dogmatics*, vol. 3, part 4, trans. A. T. MacKay, et al. (Edinburgh: T. & T. Clark, 1961), 336.

25. Charles E. Curran, *Politics, Medicine and Christian Ethics* (Philadelphia: Fortress Press, 1973), 121. As Karl Barth has stated it, the idea of the "alien dignity" of life is derived from the theological doctrine of justification: "It is a matter of the rule of the righteousness of God in Him [Christ], which, although it rules over us and applies to us, is always

a strange righteousness: *iustitia aliena*, because first and essentially it is *iustitia Christi*; and only as such *nostra, mea iustitia.*" Quoted from *Church Dogmatics*, vol. 4, part 1, trans. Geoffrey W. Bromiley (Edinburgh: T. & T. Clark, 1956), 549.

26. Barth, *Church Dogmatics*, vol. 3, part 4, 340.

27. Talcott Parsons, "Health and Disease: A Sociological and Action Perspective," in *Encyclopedia of Bioethics*, ed. Warren T. Reich (New York: Free Press, 1978), vol. 2, 591.

28. Daniel Callahan, "The WHO Definition of Health," *The Hastings Center Studies*, vol. 1, no. 3 (1973), 77–88; F. C. Redlich, "Reflections on the Concept of Health and Disease," *The Journal of Medicine and Philosophy* 1:3 (September 1976): 269–87; LeRoy Walters, "In Search of Health," *The Christian Century* 95:34 (October 25, 1978): 1014–15.

29. Stuart J. Kingma, "A Unified View of Healing," *Contact* (Geneva: Christian Medical Commission, World Council of Churches), no. 71 (December 1982): 11.

FROM GENESIS TO GENETICS

1. Liebe F. Cavalieri, *The Double-Edged Helix: Science in the Real World* (New York: Columbia University Press, 1981), 17.

2. United States Supreme Court, *Diamond v. Chakravarty* (June 16, 1980).

3. Well-considered warnings against modifying human germ cells are made in the report of the World Council of Churches' Committee on Church and Society, *Manipulating Life* (Geneva: WCC, 1982), 6–8. A comprehensive evaluation of this and related issues is found in Sheldon Krimsky, *Genetic Alchemy* (Cambridge: MIT Press, 1982).

4. For an analysis and criticism of recent thinking about eugenics see J. Robert Nelson, *Science and Our Troubled Conscience* (Philadelphia: Fortress Press, 1980), 96–117.

5. World Council of Churches, *Manipulating Life*, 29.

6. Cautionary recommendations which stop short of full regulation over experimental and commercial procedures of gene splicing are made by the United States President's Commission for the Study of Ethical Problems in Medicine and Biomedical and Behavioral Research, *Splicing Life* (Washington, D.C.: U.S. Government Printing Office, 1982).

INDEXES

INDEX OF SUBJECTS

INDEX OF NAMES

INDEX OF SCRIPTURE